The Renaissance and Reformation

A HISTORY IN DOCUMENTS

The Renaissance
and Reformation

A HISTORY IN DOCUMENTS

Merry Wiesner-Hanks

New York   Oxford
OXFORD UNIVERSITY PRESS

General Editors

Sarah Deutsch
Professor of History
Duke University

Carol K. Karlsen
Professor of History
University of Michigan

Robert G. Moeller
Professor of History
University of California, Irvine

Jeffrey N. Wasserstrom
Professor of History
University of California, Irvine

Cover: Procession of the Catholic League on the Place de Grève in Paris, from a late sixteenth century painting.

Frontispiece: A church festival, from a sixteenth-century German engraving.

Title page: The marriage of the Biblical figures Mary and Joseph, as depicted in a fifteenth-century Italian illuminated manuscript.

Oxford University Press, Inc., publishes works that further
Oxford University's objective of excellence
in research, scholarship, and education.

Oxford New York
Auckland   Cape Town   Dar es Salaam   Hong Kong   Karachi
Kuala Lumpur   Madrid   Melbourne   Mexico City   Nairobi
New Delhi   Shanghai   Taipei   Toronto

With offices in
Argentina   Austria   Brazil   Chile   Czech Republic   France   Greece
Guatemala   Hungary   Italy   Japan   Poland   Portugal   Singapore
South Korea   Switzerland   Thailand   Turkey   Ukraine   Vietnam

For titles covered by Section 112 of the US Higher Education Opportunity Act,
please visit www.oup.com/us/he for the latest information about pricing
and alternative formats.

Published by Oxford University Press, Inc.
198 Madison Avenue, New York, New York 10016
www.oup.com

Oxford is a registered trademark of Oxford University Press

Library of Congress Cataloging-in-Publication Data
Wiesner, Merry E.
  The Renaissance and Reformation : a history in documents / Merry Wiesner-Hanks.
     p. cm.
  Includes index.
  ISBN 978-0-19-533802-7 (pbk. : alk. paper)—ISBN 978-0-19-530889-1 (hard-
cover : alk. paper)
  1. Renaissance. 2. Reformation. 3. Renaissance—Sources. 4. Reformation—
Sources. I. Title.
  CB359.W44 2011
  940.2'1—dc22

                                                                    2011007316

Printing number: 9 8 7 6 5 4 3 2

Printed in the United States of America
on acid-free paper

Contents

What Is a Document?

To the historian, a document is, quite simply, any sort of historical evidence. It is a primary source, the raw material of history. A document may be more than the expected government paperwork, such as a treaty or passport. It is also a letter, diary, will, grocery list, newspaper article, recipe, memoir, oral history, school yearbook, map, chart, architectural plan, poster, musical score, play script, novel, political cartoon, painting, photograph—even an object.

Using primary sources allows us not just to read *about* history, but to read history itself. It allows us to immerse ourselves in the look and feel of an era gone by, to understand its people and their language, whether verbal or visual. And it allows us to take an active, hands-on role in (re)constructing history.

Using primary sources requires us to use our powers of detection to ferret out the relevant facts and to draw conclusions from them; just as Agatha Christie uses the scores in a bridge game to determine the identity of a murderer, the historian uses facts from a variety of sources—some, perhaps, seemingly inconsequential—to build a historical case.

The poet W. H. Auden wrote that history was the study of questions. Primary sources force us to ask questions—and then, by answering them, to construct a narrative or an argument that makes sense to us. Moreover, as we draw on the many sources from "the dust-bin of history," we can endow that narrative with character, personality, and texture—all the elements that make history so endlessly intriguing.

Cartoon

This political cartoon addresses the issue of church and state. It illustrates the Supreme Court's role in balancing the demands of the 1st Amendment of the Constitution and the desires of the religious population.

Illustration

Illustrations from children's books, such as this alphabet from the *New England Primer*, tell us how children were educated and also what the religious and moral values of the time were.

Treaty

A government document such as this 1805 treaty can reveal not only the details of government policy, but also information about the people who signed it. Here, the Indians' names were written in English transliteration by U.S. officials; the Indians added pictographs to the right of their names.

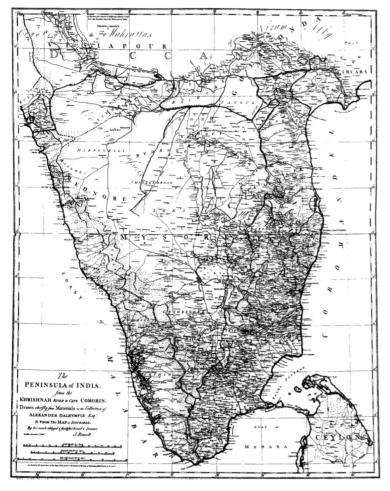

Map

A 1788 British map of India shows the region prior to British colonization, an indication of the kingdoms and provinces whose ethnic divisions would resurface later in India's history.

Object

In this fifteenth-century ewer, both the physical materials of brass and silver and the iconic depiction of heaven as a forest display the refinement of the owner, an Egyptian sultan's wife. Objects, along with manuscripts and printed materials, provide evidence about the past.

How to Read a Document

Whatever the era and subject, some very basic questions must be asked about any primary source: Who wrote or made it? What was the intended audience? In what context was it produced? Is the source trustworthy? How does the author's perspective shape the document? The answers to these questions can sometimes be found in the source itself, but many times can only be answered by comparing one document to another, to see if other pieces of evidence support the first.

A huge variety of documents is available for the era covered in this book: letters, merchants' account books, scientific treatises, memoirs, sermons, hymns, laws, poetry, portraits, drawings, buildings, household objects, and many others. The majority of the written documents come from people at the top of the social scale, who were able to read and write, but a few come from more ordinary men and women, whose words were written down by others. The historians who discovered these documents—in archives, attics, storerooms, churches, and many other places—had specialized skills to read them in their original form, but they still began with the same basic questions just outlined.

The two documents on the facing page were very common during the era of the Renaissance and the Reformation: a portrait and a legal record. During the fifteenth and sixteenth centuries, increasing numbers of wealthy and prominent people paid artists to paint their portraits. At the same time, city governments, rulers, and church officials established courts where people charged with various crimes appeared. The written records of their trials are one of the few places where we can "hear" the voices of those who could not read and write.

Subject

This portrait of Pope Leo X and two of his nephews who were cardinals was painted in oil by Raphael, the most sought-after artist in Europe. Painted portraits were staged in a certain way, often through a conversation between the subject—who was generally paying for the portrait—and the artist. Unsurprisingly, portraits often show subjects as they wished to be remembered, not the way they actually looked.

Composition and Body Language

Renaissance portraitists usually followed certain artistic rules in composing paintings—the main subject was in the middle and the lines of the portrait led the viewers' eye to that subject. Here Raphael follows these rules, and suggests the pope's power through other aspects of the painting as well, including his velvet robe and cap—deep red in the actual painting—and the way the cardinals stand behind him. Leo's hand on the book in front of him is an indication of his power to interpret religious texts for all Christians. His puffy face and serious expression do not seem to be idealized, however, and some art historians have seen in his appearance a recognition that criticism of the Catholic Church was growing stronger right at the time this portrait was painted.

The Court

Religious reformers in the sixteenth century established various types of courts to try to force people to believe what they viewed as the correct interpretation of Christian teachings and to live moral and pious lives. In the Swiss city of Geneva, the Protestant reformer John Calvin oversaw a special court called the consistory, which kept extensive records of all its activities. Here, a cobbler named Jacques Bornant is summoned to appear before the consistory and charged with gambling and not attending church.

Defense

Bornant answers that he does, in fact, go to sermons on Sundays, and provides further evidence of his religious devotion by reciting the Lord's Prayer and the confession, a short statement of faith. As a poor tradesman, he would have learned the Lord's Prayer and the Calvinist statement of faith orally, the first perhaps as a child from his parents, and the second just recently, because Geneva had only been Calvinist for about a year at the time Bornant was summoned before the consistory.

Verdict

The officials of the consistory set a relatively easy punishment for Bonant's misbehavior, simply scolding him and telling him to shape up. This suggests that this was the first time that he had been brought in, for punishments set for repeat offenders, or for those accused of more serious crimes, included whipping, imprisonment, and banishment from the city.

Excerpt from the Registers of the Geneva Consistory, 1542

Jacques Bornant, called Callaz, cobbler

Summoned because of absence from the sermons and wasting time in gambling games. Answers that he goes to the sermons on Sundays. Said the Lord's prayer and the confession but does not know the ten commandments. The consistory advises that he be admonished to cease to gamble to give an example to others, and to frequent the sermons.

Introduction
Rebirths and Reformations

Reflecting on the "perfect design, divine grace . . . and absolute perfection" he saw in the art of Florence and other Italian cities, the sixteenth-century painter, architect, and writer Giorgio Vasari coined a new word to describe this artistic movement—"Renaissance," which means "rebirth." At about the same time in Germany, the emperor ordered political leaders who had adopted the religious ideas of Martin Luther to return to obedience to the pope, the emperor's ally. The German princes issued a formal protest of this order, giving a name to the movement of religious reform sweeping Germany—the "Protestant Reformation." Over the last five hundred years, these two words, Renaissance and Reformation, have broadened beyond the worlds of art and religion to be used as a sort of shorthand to describe the era of European history from about 1400 to about 1600.

Although Vasari was the first to use the word *Renaissance* in print, he was not the first to feel that something was being reborn. Two centuries earlier, the Florentine poet and scholar Francesco Petrarch spent long hours searching for classical Latin manuscripts in dusty monastery libraries and wandering around the many ruins of the Roman Empire remaining in Italy. He became obsessed with the classical past, and felt that the writers and artists of ancient Rome had reached a level of perfection in their work that had not since been duplicated. Writers of his own day should follow these ancient models, thought Petrarch, and ignore the thousand-year period

1

Giorgio Vasari's self-portrait was printed in his book describing the literary references he had worked into the rooms that he decorated in the city hall of Florence. Self-portraits became much more common in the Renaissance than they had been earlier, as artists sought to demonstrate their individual talents and convey their distinct personalities. Here Vasari portrays himself surrounded by classical figures representing architecture, painting, and sculpture, all arts that he had mastered.

between his own time and that of Rome, which he saw as a "dark" age during which people had written bad Latin and built "Gothic" cathedrals—so named because they were so disunified in their style they could only have been invented by the uncouth Goths.

Petrarch clearly believed he was witnessing the dawning of a new era, in which writers and artists would recapture the glory that was Rome. He proposed a new kind of education to help them do this, in which young men would study the works of ancient Latin and Greek authors, using them as models of how to write clearly, argue effectively, and speak persuasively in contemporary society. Studying the "humanities," as this course of study was called, would provide essential skills for future diplomats, lawyers, military leaders, businessmen, and politicians, as well as writers and artists.

It would provide a much broader and more practical type of training than that offered at universities, which at the time focused on theology and philosophy or on theoretical training for lawyers and physicians. Petrarch's ideas spread, and humanist schools were established in Florence, Venice, and other Italian cities. By Vasari's time two hundred years later, humanism and its notion of a rebirth had spread across the Alps to northern Europe.

Italian artists, who had the ruins of the ancient Roman Empire all around them, began to use Roman buildings as inspiration for their own designs. They designed buildings that followed classical principles of balance and proportion, carved statues that showed realistic human forms like those of the ancient Greeks and Romans, and painted portraits that brought out their subjects' personality. Both art and literature celebrated the beauty of the natural world and the distinctiveness and talents of creative individuals. Some thought that the products of their own day had actually gone beyond the classical originals. Vasari was one of these, writing, "Many works today are more perfect and better finished than were those of the great masters of the past."

The Renaissance was thus a wide-reaching change in style and attitude and not a single historical event, which means that it "happened" at different times in different parts of Europe. Roughly, we can say it began in Italy in the fourteenth century; spread to France, Germany, and Spain by the end of the fifteenth century; to England by the early part of the sixteenth century; and to Scandinavia in the seventeenth century. "Renaissance" is used to describe fifteenth-century Italian paintings, sixteenth-century English literature, and seventeenth-century Scandinavian architecture. William Shakespeare is considered a Renaissance writer, although he lived 250 years after Petrarch.

The Reformation is both an event and an era. In the early part of the sixteenth century, a number of people, including some who had been educated as humanists, thought that the Christian church in Western Europe, headed by the pope in Rome, needed reform. (The Christian church centered in Rome is usually called Catholic—a word that means worldwide—or Roman Catholic.) It owned about one quarter of the land, and higher officials, including bishops who were in charge of specific regions, and the pope, often came from noble families and lived lavishly. The pope and some of the bishops were the political rulers of their territories, so they sponsored armies and made and enforced laws just like kings did. People paid taxes directly to the church to support their local priest and the hierarchy of higher officials. They also made donations to monasteries and convents, where monks and nuns who had made special vows said prayers and carried out ceremonies, and gave money to friars, men who took religious vows but preached, taught, and assisted those in need outside of monasteries.

Most people attended church, went on pilgrimages, prayed, participated in religious processions, and carried out a number of other activities to help achieve salvation or ask God's blessing and protection. Their strong piety was sometimes accompanied by dissatisfaction with the church, however. Many people thought that the pope and bishops had too much power, and that they gained money by leading people to believe that donations alone, without faith, would get them into heaven. They criticized the way that church taxes were used, and believed that many priests, monks, nuns, and friars did not live up to their vows but instead were worldly and immoral. Some said that the pope's supreme authority in the church was not based on the Bible, that the church should give up its wealth, and that the prayers of priests or monks were no more powerful than those of ordinary Christians. Criticism and calls for reform had been around for centuries, but they grew louder in the early sixteenth century.

The Florentine sculptor Baccio Bandinelli commissioned this engraving of his workshop in 1550 to publicize his accomplishments and aspirations. In this idealized view, art is an intellectual enterprise in which well-dressed men calmly study classical statues and human bones. In reality, a sculptor's workshop would have been filled with noise and dust.

Martin Luther, a sixteenth-century friar and professor of theology at the German university of Wittenberg, was one of the loudest and most effective voices calling for reform. Just as Petrarch and Vasari looked to the writers and artists of the classical past for models, Luther looked to the apostles of the New Testament and the practices of the early church. He and other Protestant reformers, such as John Calvin in Switzerland, thought that the Bible alone, and not the traditions of the church, was the source for true Christian teachings. They rejected the authority of the pope and the privileged legal status of priests, and believed no one should take special vows or live in monasteries, but should instead get married and live in families, serving God through their work or family life. People should go to church and pray, but pray directly to God or Jesus, not to the Virgin Mary or the saints, who might have been good people but had no special powers or claim to holiness. Although there were differences among the reformers, Protestants all stressed that faith given by God, and not good works, was the key to salvation. They thought that religious services and the Bible should be in the languages people spoke, instead of Latin, which could only be learned in school and thus was known to only a few.

People in Luther's Germany and then other parts of Europe accepted the Protestant message. This included rulers of territories, who dismissed priests and bishops loyal to the pope and hired Protestant pastors in their place. The Catholic Church responded by reforming some of the practices that had been most criticized. It improved education for priests, demanded higher standards of moral conduct, and ended the selling of church positions. This Catholic Reformation did not bring a change in basic teachings, however. For Catholics, the pope was still clearly the head of the church, monks and nuns had a special role, saints were to be honored, and long-established traditions, along with the Bible, transmitted true Christian teachings.

The educational reforms and cultural changes of the Renaissance spread gradually and generally peacefully. Universities sometimes opposed the new style of learning, but their objections did not prevent the opening of humanist academies. Some artists and their patrons continued to favor older artistic styles, but this did not stop other artists from using new techniques or forms when they painted portraits or designed buildings. In contrast, the Reformation led to more than a century of religious war, as Protestant and Catholic armies battled in Switzerland, Germany, France, and other areas. Western Europe had known only one official Christian church for more than a millennium, and most people could not imagine different Christian churches coexisting peacefully. Rulers, even those who became Protestant, did not want to allow different varieties of Christianity within their own territories, and forbade people from Christian groups other than their own to worship. Sometimes they arrested and killed them. The threat of persecution led people to migrate to places where their religious ideas matched those of the rulers, leaving their homes and property behind.

Religious differences were not the only force causing people to travel or move, as the opportunity for wealth was also a powerful motive. Great riches came primarily through trade, and by the late fourteenth century, long-distance voyages by Indian, Malay, Arab, and

Italian sailors and merchants linked the Mediterranean, Indian Ocean, and South China Sea. In the fifteenth century, ventures by the Chinese and then by the Portuguese widened this trading network further. Spanish, Portuguese, and English voyages in the sixteenth century connected the Atlantic and Pacific into this web of trade, as spices, precious metals, and other goods were bought and sold globally.

Overseas explorations and the colonies founded as a result of these explorations eventually transformed Europe into the dominant power in the world. Voyages to the New World posed an intellectual challenge for Renaissance thinkers, however, as they were suddenly confronted with lands and peoples that had been unknown to their classical idols. Religious leaders generally saw these new lands as an opportunity rather than a problem, sending missionaries to win converts to Christianity, building churches, and establishing institutions such as schools and courts to teach and enforce Christian ideas and practices.

The Renaissance and the Reformation are often seen as opposing movements because Renaissance humanists celebrated things of this world such as beauty and friendship, whereas Protestant and Catholic reformers emphasized eternal salvation and the life to come. This overstates the differences, however. Many humanists regarded spiritual concerns as important, and many reformers praised God's handiwork in the world around them. The new learning of the Renaissance, especially the study of ancient languages, contributed to calls for religious change.

The Renaissance and Reformation are also parallel movements. Both Renaissance artists and Reformation pastors originally wanted a return to what they viewed as a golden age of the past, but eventually created something very new. Both, we might say, began as rebirths, but became reformations, devising new artistic styles, new types of literature, and new understandings of the proper relations between humans and their God. European exploration and colonization fits this pattern as well, beginning as an attempt to claim a place in long-established trading networks, but ending in the establishment of new and much larger sets of connections.

For centuries people have seen these three developments— the Renaissance, the Reformation, and the European voyages of discovery—as the beginning of the "modern" world. Indeed, it was Renaissance humanists who first divided their history into three parts: ancient, medieval, and modern. As the modern era gets longer and longer, however, the Renaissance and Reformation recede further into the past. Continuities between these eras and the Middle

Ages that preceded them seem more apparent to us than they did to someone like Vasari who was so aware (and so proud) of what was new. The documents that follow will allow you to assess both changes and continuities in this era, to see how artists, reformers, and rulers, but also more ordinary men and women, shaped their world, and our own.

Note on Sources and Interpretation

The history of the Renaissance and the Reformation began to be written during these periods themselves. Many humanists were historians, and wrote multivolume surveys of the rise and fall of ancient Rome or the rise of their own city. Vasari actually used the word "Renaissance" for the first time in a historical work, an examination of the lives of artists in Italy from the thirteenth century to his own day. Religious reformers also wrote histories, connecting their calls for change to the story of the church in its earliest centuries.

Both humanists and reformers described their goals in writing history and in the broader intellectual changes they were seeking with the Latin phrase *ad fontes*, which means "to the sources." (*Fons* in Latin also means spring or fountain, both of which are sources of water.) They thought that true knowledge depended on going back to the oldest and most fundamental sources, the Greek and Latin classics in the case of humanists and the Bible in the case of religious reformers. Interpretations of the Renaissance and Reformation have changed over the centuries, but the idea that history should be based on original sources has not. In fact, the format of this book is based on just this idea: Everyone studying history should read original sources, which give more direct access to the lives of people in earlier times than do secondary studies, and allow each reader to draw independent conclusions.

The sources in this book range far beyond those that historians in the fifteenth and sixteenth centuries (or even the nineteenth and much of the twentieth centuries) would have used, because the idea of what history is has changed. History in earlier centuries was primarily a political and military story, with kings, generals, presidents, statesmen, and their advisors as the main actors. Intellectual history was sometimes woven into this, because the ideas of major religious leaders, philosophers, and scientists were seen as important and often had an impact on political developments. Thus from the Renaissance to the middle of the twentieth century, historians relied primarily on official documents, the published works and letters of great men, and other written sources that gave insight into the lives of the prominent and powerful. Such sources remain important, but since the 1960s historians and people interested in history have become more concerned with the lives of ordinary people of the past, that is, with people like themselves. They increasingly examine all aspects of human experience, not just politics, and all types of people, including women, children, and common men. Thus social and cultural history have joined political, military, and intellectual history, and the scope of materials used to study the past has broadened significantly. Ordinary people show up in official documents most often when they have done something judged wrong by those in power: not paid their taxes, fought with their neighbors, spoken against the government. Until the twentieth century—and in some parts of the world until today—most people could not read and write, so they left no written records of their own. To study the social and cultural history of the Renaissance and Reformation, then, historians use family records, business contracts, books written for children, women's letters, household inventories, merchants' memoirs, and epitaphs on tombstones. They examine material objects as well as written documents, for even men and women who were not literate shaped and responded to the world around them through the houses they constructed, the clothing they sewed, and the furniture and other objects they made and decorated.

This broadening in scope and sources has led to new interpretations of this era. Historians writing during the Renaissance emphasized the many ways their own times broke with the centuries that came before, and historians writing in the eighteenth and nineteenth centuries largely agreed with them, viewing the Renaissance as the forerunner to their own even more enlightened times. They highlighted the power of secular ideals and beliefs in individualism. More recently, historians have noted that religious values remained extremely important to even the most highly educated men, and that family and group connections remained strong. Other historians have also pointed out that Renaissance advances were not open to all. "Did women have a Renaissance?" asked one historian during the 1970s, who answered her question with a resounding "No," although some more recent historians have answered it with "Well, maybe a few did." Research into the lives of other social groups, such as peasants or urban workers, has yielded similar judgments.

Historians looking at the impact of the Renaissance in a global perspective have also modified their interpretations. The European voyages were earlier described as heroic ventures in which fearless individuals broke with traditional ways of thinking and discovered new lands. Columbus is still regarded as pretty fearless, but we now recognize that he was motivated to a large degree by religious aims, that many people in the Mediterranean area had long known the world was round, that his treatment of the peoples he encountered was hardly heroic, and that these lands were "discovered" only from the point of view of Europeans, not those who already lived there. Thus historians studying the Renaissance in Europe have tended to point out that its impact was more limited than earlier scholars claimed, and those studying the world that its impact was more negative.

Changing interpretations of the Reformation have followed a similar path. The earliest historians of the Reformation—including some reformers themselves—wrote with a strong confessional bias. Thus to Protestant historians Luther was a hero who had rescued Christianity from the evils of papal greed and corruption, whereas to Catholic historians he was a villain or a buffoon who had been motivated by his own lust and desire for power. This polarized view continued into the twentieth century, and to it was added a Marxist interpretation that saw the Reformation largely in economic terms, as part of the rise of capitalism. Over the last fifty years or so, most historians have attempted to go beyond a confessional point of view and developed a more balanced perspective. Like historians of the Renaissance, they have stressed continuities as well as changes, paying more attention to earlier reform movements and the ways in which Protestants built on these. Historians of the Reformation now point out the similarities between Protestant and Catholic ideas and institutions in the sixteenth century and beyond. Using a much wider range of sources than had earlier historians, they study the religious ideas of ordinary men and women, and the actual impact of Reformation teachings on their lives. They note that people did not simply accept or reject new religious ideas and practices, but selectively adopted, modified, and blended them. Many historians of the Reformation increasingly look beyond Europe, analyzing ways in which people living in Africa, Asia, and the Americas understood Christian teachings and transformed them during the process of conversion, creating new forms of Christianity.

New sources and new interpretations have deepened our understanding of both the Renaissance and the Reformation. Their legacy has become more complex and more problematic, but this reassessment has not lessened their importance as shapers of the modern world.

nstueran du
ley conuoit
pur dun xxn
de dy fraucoie
isuent dtles
loque et furent troie battaille
de leure gene Cn la pme
re fuent une huit cene ba
cbuietz quattre mulle archies
et quuse cene arballeftruar

Et dcefte auant ffard fu
rent dnefz le conneftable
les duez deleane et de bout
bon les conte du et de Ri
cbemont et plibeure aul
tre bone capitaine lecote
de Vendofme et autree offi
ciere du roy furent ozdonne
a faire vue efle atout quuse
cene bonnnee duuuee vout

CHAPTER 1

The Tumultuous Late Middle Ages

French and English forces collide in 1415 at Agincourt, a battle in the Hundred Years' War. The French artist of this manuscript from the late fifteenth century shows both sides carrying long pikes. Several English soldiers in the middle carry longbows, the weapon that was primarily responsible for the English victory in this battle.

Francesco Petrarch, the first to describe his times as the dawning of a new era, looked to the classical past for inspiration, and termed the period between the fall of the ancient Roman Empire and his own day as the Dark Ages. To most Europeans living when Petrarch did, however, that label was more appropriate for their own era. During the eleventh through the thirteenth century—a period historians term the "High Middle Ages"—cities grew, trade increased, population expanded, and people established new institutions. The High Middle Ages are usually described in glowing terms, as "vital," or "vibrant," or "vigorous," symbolized by the soaring cathedrals built in scores of cities. By contrast, words used to describe the fourteenth and early fifteenth centuries— a period historians term the Late Middle Ages—are usually negative: "decline," "crisis," or even "calamitous."

The calamities began with climate change. The High Middle Ages had been a period of warmer than usual temperatures, but beginning around 1300, the European climate became colder and wetter. Rivers froze, and crops did not ripen or were ruined in torrential rains. Europeans had expanded their croplands in the High Middle Ages and were farming land on which the soil was too poor to grow the grains on which people and animals depended for food. Much of this land had lost its fertility by the fourteenth century, which combined with the worsening climate to cause crop failures. Bad harvests led to famine, sometimes localized and sometimes widespread. Famine resulted in population decline as deaths outnumbered births and people became less resistant to disease.

In 1347 the introduction of a new epidemic disease into Europe dramatically speeded up the decrease in population. Most historians and epidemiologists identify this as the bubonic plague, caused by the bacillus Yersinia pestis, *a disease that normally afflicts rats. Fleas living on the infected rats drink their blood, and then pass the bacteria that cause the plague on to the next rat they bite. Usually the disease is limited to rats and other rodents, but at certain points in history—perhaps when most rats have been killed off—the fleas have jumped from their rodent hosts to humans and other animals. One of these times appears to have occurred in the Eastern Roman Empire in the sixth century, when a plague killed millions of people, and another was in China and India in the 1890s, when millions also died. Our understanding of bubonic plague comes primarily from this later outbreak, and recently some historians have pointed out that there were significant differences between this outbreak and that of the fourteenth century. They question whether the fourteenth-century outbreak was actually not the bubonic plague, but a different disease, perhaps something like the Ebola virus. Medical historians are using new research methods, such as studying the tooth pulp from bodies in plague cemeteries to see if it contains DNA remains of bubonic plague bacteria, to investigate the medical side of the plague in more detail.*

Whatever the disease was that devastated Europe, it emerged first in western China. It would probably have remained a small-scale local outbreak had there not been relatively safe trade routes across Asia crossing the vast Mongol Empire. Merchant caravans carrying silk, spices, and gold carried the disease westward, and so did armies. In 1346, Tartar armies besieged the city of Kaffa on the Black Sea, a port controlled by the Italian city of Genoa. The besiegers were nearly successful when they began to die in great numbers, and as they retreated—so the story goes—they catapulted plague-infected corpses over the city walls. The plague spread in the crowded city, and several Genoese ships hurried home, hoping to escape. From Italy, the plague spread throughout Europe. By the end of 1348, it had crossed the English Channel, and by the end of 1350, it had reached northern Sweden. Between one quarter and one third of the population of Europe died in this first outbreak, with only a few isolated areas or cities that adopted very strict quarantine measures spared. Subsequent outbreaks were never as deadly as the first one, but plague stayed for centuries, joining other diseases to make a recovery of preplague population levels slow in coming.

Physicians could offer little to combat the plague, and many people thought the disease was a punishment sent by God. Artists created, and people bought, paintings and woodcuts with images of sin and death—skeletons dancing or leading people off to an unknown fate. Some groups recommended more extreme demonstrations of guilt and repentance, beating themselves and marching from town to town urging others to join them. These groups, called flagellants, often grew into unruly mobs. City and government officials worried about where their violence might lead, and eventually the pope ordered an army to disband the flagellants.

Most people did not respond to the plague with extreme behavior, but combined religious belief, folk magic, and medicine. They said prayers asking God to spare them, went on pilgrimages to holy places, avoided people who were already infected, wore good luck charms to protect themselves, and hoped for an afterlife without disease. As is often true with devastating events, the plague highlighted central qualities of medieval society: deep religious feeling, suspicion of those who were different, and a view of the world shaped largely by oral tradition, with a bit of classical knowledge mixed in among the educated elite.

Famine, disease, war, and violence all marked the Late Middle Ages, even more than they did most eras of human history. To many people, the most appropriate symbol for their own era was the "dance of death," in which skeletons led people of all social classes to an open grave. Despite deep pessimism, however, people also sought to improve their lot here on earth and work toward a place in heaven. Revolts by peasants and workers are one example of this, for they represent poorer people's attempts to gain a larger share of the prosperity open to Europe's smaller postplague population.

The Black Death

The Genoese ships that fled the plague at Kaffa instead carried the disease with them, as the Italian official Gabriele de Mussi reported in dramatic language in a chronicle of the early spread of the plague written in 1348. As Mussi comments, the plague spread directly from person to person as well as through flea bites. This direct human transmission is one of the factors that have led some historians to wonder whether the fourteenth-century plague might not have been bubonic plague. They also point to the speed with which the plague spread, and the fact that there are no reports of large-scale rat die-offs.

O Genoa, what thou hast done, since we of Genoa and Venice are compelled to make God's chastisement manifest. Alas! Our ships enter the port, but of a thousand sailors hardly ten are spared. We

Die ist als got moyses.jnes dz er alten nem vnder des kunges he
mit vnd die vff wurst dez geschach.wo wurst die lur tegupt
voll sullen vn plaingen vō gottes rich:.

Die ist vō der nachte figt als got
moyses zu pharao schiket.Dm er sin
volk lieszom·yoder om hagel wurd ke·
vich des vubldes vnrecht men:.
hies got aber sinen knet
Gan bi den selben tagen
Ze pharaone vnd im sage
Das er sin lute im so lie lan
Wolt aber er der werschaft widerstan
So solt er sprechen fürbas
Got der herre spricket das
Lass min lute nu voru von dir
Daz si ir opher bringend mir
Thust du des mt so wil ich
die schleg vn zlagen gar senden vb dich
Die dem lande sind geschehen
Vnd wil an dir lassen sehen
min sterki vnd min kraft
Daz an dir werde namhaft
min name vnd werd och wit er kant
Vnd das über alli lant
sin name der welte werd kunt

morgen ze dirre selben stunt
Egnen ich den grösten hagel hie
Der noch ze den ziten ie
menschen ögen ward erkant
So dm hie buhast wart das lant
Da von lauft dm vihe mit gran
Ze velde lauft es min stan
Daz es iht verdirbe
Vno von hagel sterbe
wie moyses·sin hand gen himel strackte
vnd grúlich wers kam·von hagel es
Vu was der lantlúten vil
Die mder selben tage zil
Got vorchtend vnd sinen zorn
die sich des herrend vsler korn
Die hiessend ir vihe behalten
Da hamm nan vnd es walten
Das es iht verdurbe
Oder vff dem veld sturbe
So der hagel solte komen
Ju nahe ani ende hat genomen
Vnd ward der ander tag er kant

Symptoms of the deadly bubonic plague included large swellings on the body, as in this illustration from an early fifteenth-century Bible. Here sufferers lie on pillows awaiting death, while in the background Jesus prays for them.

reach our homes; our kindred and our neighbours come from all parts to visit us. Woe to us for we cast at them the darts of death! Whilst we spoke to them, whilst they embraced us and kissed us, we scattered the poison from our lips. Going back to their homes, they in turn soon infected their whole families, who in three days succumbed, and were buried in one common grave. Priests and doctors visiting the sick returned from their duties ill, and soon were numbered with the dead.

No one disputes the plague's dreadful effects. Commentators from many parts of Europe agreed with the Italian poet Giovanni Boccaccio's description of the course of the disease in Florence, where the plague struck in 1348. He uses this to set the scene in the *Decameron,* his best known work, written during the early 1350s when the plague was still fresh in his mind. In this book, Boccaccio imagines a group of men and women who have fled Florence to escape the plague telling each other stories. The symptoms Boccaccio describes have given the plague its names: Later physicians called the swellings in the groin and armpits *buboes,* the origin of the word "bubonic," and the dark blotches might be the origin of the term "Black Death," often used for the fourteenth-century outbreak of this disease.

It began in both men and women with certain swellings either in the groin or under the armpits, some of which grew to the size of a normal apple and others to the size of an egg (more or less), and the people called them plague-boils and from the two parts of the body already mentioned, within a brief space of time, the said deadly boils began to spread indiscriminately over every part of the body; and after this, the symptoms of the illness changed to black or livid spots appearing on the arms and thighs and on every part of the body, some large ones and sometimes many little ones scattered all around. And just as the boils were originally, and still are, a very certain indication of impending death, in like manner these spots came to mean the same thing for whoever had them . . . Almost all died after the third day of the appearance of the previously described symptoms.

Reactions and Explanations

Along with the symptoms, Boccaccio's *Decameron* also describes people's various responses to the disease. Boccaccio's fictional characters were patterned after real people who left cities for the countryside, a common reaction to the plague for those who could afford it. Despite Boccaccio's comments about family members' coldness, people were saddened by the loss of their loved ones, especially their children.

There were some people who thought that living moderately and avoiding all superfluity might help a great deal in resisting this disease, and so they gathered in small groups and lived entirely apart from everyone else. Others thought the opposite: they believed that drinking too much, enjoying life, going about singing and celebrating, satisfying in every way the appetites as best one could, laughing, and making light of everything that happened was the best medicine for such a disease; so they practiced to the fullest what they believed by going from one tavern to another all day and night, drinking to excess; and often they would make merry in private homes, doing everything that pleased or amused them the most. This they were able to do easily, for everyone felt he was doomed to die and, as a result, abandoned his property. . . . The fact was that one citizen avoided another, that almost no one cared for his neighbor and that relatives rarely or hardly ever visited each other—they stayed far apart. This disaster has struck such fear into the hearts of men and women that brother abandoned brother, uncle abandoned nephew, sister left almost unbelievable—fathers and mothers neglected to tend and care for their children, as if they were not their own.

The plight of the lower class and, perhaps, a large part of the middle class was even more pathetic: most of them stayed in their homes or neighborhoods either because of their poverty or their hopes for remaining safe, and every day they fell sick by the thousands; and not having servants or attendants of any kind, they almost always died. Many ended their lives in the public streets, during the day or at

The year 1348 left us lonely. . . . The life we lead is a dream, and I wish I could have woken before this . . . . Oh happy people of the future, who have not known these miseries and perchance will class our testimony with the fables.

—1348 letter of Francesco Petrarch, grieving over his many friends who had died

Residents of the French city of Tournai bury victims of the plague in this illumination from a chronicle describing events in the city during 1349. The men at the left are working so hard to carry coffins and corpses that one even has his shirt off. The scene reflects Boccaccio's lament that plague victims were just dumped into the ground without proper mourning and funeral ceremonies.

night, while many others who died in their homes were discovered dead by the neighbors only by the smell of their decomposing bodies. The city was full of corpses. . . . Moreover, the dead were honored with no tears or candles or funeral mourners but worse: things had reached such a point that the people who died were cared for as we care for goats today. Thus, it became quite obvious that what the wise had not been able to endure with patience through the few calamities of everyday life now became a matter of indifference to even the most simple-minded people as a result of this colossal misfortune.

So many corpses would arrive in front of a church every day and at every hour that the amount of holy ground for burials was certainly insufficient for the ancient custom of giving each body its individual place; when all the graves were full, huge trenches were dug in all of the cemeteries of the churches and into them the new arrivals were dumped by the hundreds; and they were packed in there with dirt, one on top of another, like a ship's cargo, until the trench was filled.

People sought answers for why the plague was happening. In a 1348 report, the medical faculty of the University of Paris, one of the most prestigious medical schools in Europe, suggested a huge range of pos-

sible explanations, an indication that they had no idea. To their astronomical and environmental causes, they added divine will, although somewhat as an afterthought.

We say that the distant and first cause of this pestilence was and is the configuration of the heavens. In 1345, at one hour after noon on 20 March, there was a major conjunction of three planets in Aquarius. This conjunction, along with other earlier conjunctions and eclipses, by causing a deadly corruption of the air around us, signifies mortality and famine . . .

We believe that the present epidemic or plague has arisen from air corrupt in its substance . . .

And moreover these winds, which have become so common here, have carried among us (and many perhaps continue to do so in future) bad, rotten and poisonous vapours from elsewhere: from swamps, lakes, and chasms, for instance, and also (which is even more dangerous) from unburied or unburnt corpses—which might well have been a cause of the epidemic. Another possible cause of corruption, which needs to be borne in mind, is the escape of the rottenness trapped in the centre of the earth as a result of earthquakes. . . .

Unseasonable weather is a particular cause of illness . . . It is because the whole year here—or most of it—was warm and wet that the air is pestilential.

Plagues are likely, although not inevitable, because so many exhalations and inflammations have been observed, such as a comet and shooting stars. Also the sky has looked yellow and the air reddish because of the burnt vapours.

We must not overlook the fact that any pestilence proceeds from the divine will, and our advice can therefore only be to return humbly to God.

Suggestions for ways to combat or prevent the plague were similarly wide-ranging. If the plague came from poisoned air, people reasoned, then strong-smelling herbs or other substances, like rosemary, juniper, or sulfur, held in front of the nose or burned as incense, might stop it. Medicines made from plants that were bumpy or that oozed liquid might work, keeping the more dangerous swellings and oozings of the plague away. One fifteenth-century treatise centered on ridding the body of bad fluids through vomiting, sweating, or bloodletting. These methods were ineffective.

During the pestilence everyone over seven should be made to vomit daily from an empty stomach, and twice a week, or more often if necessary, he should lie well wrapped up in a warm bed and drink

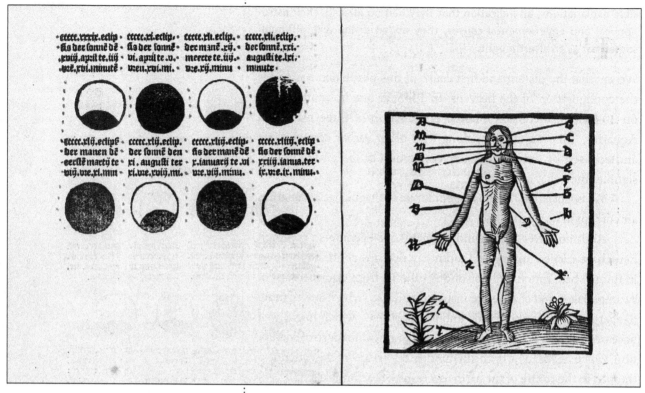

The most common treatment for any type of illness in Europe until the seventeenth century was taking blood from a vein, for which this sixteenth-century medical manual provides guidance. Surgeons used leeches, knives, and sharpened glass cups, and sometimes varied their procedures according to the phases of the moon, as the manual here suggests.

warm ale with ginger so that he sweats copiously, and he should never touch the sheets after that until they have been cleansed of the sweat, for if the person sweating had been in contact with the pestilence a healthy man could catch the plague from the sheets unless they have been well washed. As soon as he feels an itch or pricking in his flesh he must use a goblet or cupping horn to let blood and draw down the blood from the heart, and this should be done two or three times at intervals of one or two days at most. And if he should feel himself oppressed deep within his body, then he should let blood in the nearest veins, either in the arms or in the main veins of the feet.

Religion and the Plague

While doctors focused on environmental causes and medical treatments, other commentators focused on God, who they thought must be punishing people for terrible sins. Priests and preachers recommended spiritual remedies, as in this fourteenth-century sermon by Theophilus of Milan, a Benedictine monk.

Whenever anyone is struck down by the plague they should immediately provide themselves with a medicine like this. Let him first

Dressed in the clothes of a physician, St. Sebastian, who people viewed as protecting them from the plague, lances a woman's neck-swelling, while others line up to be treated. This French painting shows one of the medical treatments offered by doctors, but suggests that it will not be successful, for above the doctor an angel and devil both stand ready to snatch the woman's soul when she dies.

gather as much as he can of bitter loathing towards the sins committed by him, and the same quantity of true contrition of the heart, and mix the two into an ointment with the water of tears. Then let him make a vomit of frank and honest confession, by which he shall be purged of the pestilential poison of sin, and the boil of his vices shall be totally liquefied and melt away. Then the spirit, formerly weighed down by the plague of sin, will be left all light and full of blessed joy. Afterwards let him take the most delightful and precious medicine: the body of our lord and saviour Jesus Christ.

Along with looking for medical or spiritual causes and cures, people also searched for scapegoats. They often focused on Jews, against whom accusations often appeared during times of crisis. Jean de Venette, a French monk relating the events of the late 1340s in his chronicle, described massacres of Jewish communities at the time of the plague, which were the largest persecutions of Jews in Europe between the eleventh and the twentieth centuries.

The infection, and the sudden death which it brought, were blamed on the Jews, who were said to have poisoned wells and rivers and corrupted the air. Accordingly the whole world brutally rose against them and in Germany and in other countries which had Jewish communities many thousands were indiscriminately butchered, slaughtered and burnt alive by the Christians. The constancy shown by them and their wives was amazing. When Jews were being burnt

This stone is a memorial
That a later generation may know
That 'neath it lies hidden a pleasant bud,
A cherished child.
Perfect in knowledge,
A reader of the Bible . . .
Though only fifteen years in age,
He was like a man of eighty in knowledge . . .
He died of the plague . . .
And the father is left, sad and aching.
May the God of heaven
Grant him comfort.

—Epitaph for a Jewish boy who died of the plague in 1349 in the city of Toledo, Spain mothers would throw their own children into the flames rather than risk them being baptised, and would then hurl themselves into the fire after them, to burn with their husbands and children.

Economic and Social Effects

Over the long run, those who survived the plague had things a bit better. With fewer mouths to feed, each person got more and better food and clothing. Peasant farms became slightly larger, and peasants responded to the drop in population by experimenting with more efficient ways of doing things. They tried new crops that took fewer people to plant and harvest, or switched to raising cattle, sheep, or horses, because these required even less labor. They used new tools and more machinery, especially windmills and water mills for grinding grain or sawing wood.

To many observers, such as Jean de Venette, it seemed as if the dead were being quickly replaced.

When the epidemic was over the men and women still alive married each other. Everywhere women conceived more readily than usual. None proved barren, on the contrary, there were pregnant

A woodcut illustration from an early French printed book shows scenes of work in the countryside for each of the twelve signs of the zodiac. Scenes of everyday life in the different seasons of the year were often used to indicate the passing of time, and provide evidence about the lives of ordinary people that is often missing from written sources.

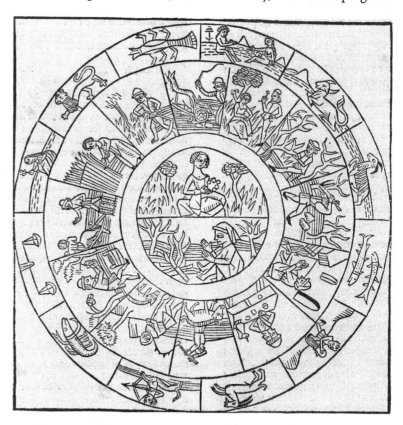

women wherever you looked. Several gave birth to twins, and some to living triplets.

Even twins or triplets—if, indeed, there were more than usual—could not make up for the huge drop in population, however. Workers knew they were in short supply, and demanded higher wages and higher prices for their products, a situation de Venette also noted.

What was also amazing was that, in spite of there being plenty of everything, it was all twice as expensive: household equipment and foodstuffs, as well as merchandise, hired labour, farm workers and servants. The only exception was property and houses, of which there is a glut to this day . . . . After the plague men became more miserly and grasping, although many owned more than they had before. They were also more greedy and quarrelsome, involving themselves in brawls, disputes, and lawsuits.

City and national governments all over Europe tried to freeze wages and prices at their preplague levels. In 1349, King Edward III of England issued a proclamation to that effect, which was affirmed by Parliament several years later as the Statute of Laborers. Those who refused to hire themselves out were to be put in jail, and urban workers such as carpenters, smiths, butchers, and bakers who charged too much for their

Farmers bring grain to be milled at waterwheels along the Seine River in Paris, carrying it up ladders to the grinding stones powered by falling water. The artist of this illustration from a fourteenth-century manuscript shows the vats into which flour flowed through the windows of the mill. Mills such as this were an increasingly common sight along rivers and streams.

products were to be fined. Mayors and other officials who did not enforce this were themselves to be fined, as was anyone who gave money to what the statute called "sturdy beggars," those who lawmakers saw as capable of work.

In this manuscript illustration, a juggler spins a plate on a stick, while an acrobat does a handstand and a young musician plays a drum. Groups of entertainers traveled from town to town in many parts of Europe, performing plays and putting on shows for a small fee, giving people some relief from their long days of work.

Because a great part of the people, and especially of workmen and servants, have lately died in the pestilence, many seeing the necessities of masters and great scarcity of servants, will not serve unless they may receive excessive wages, and others preferring to beg in idleness rather than by labor to get their living; we, considering the grievous incommodities which of the lack especially of plowmen and such laborers may hereafter come, have upon deliberation and treaty with the prelates and the nobles and learned men assisting us, with their unanimous counsel ordained:

That every man and woman of our realm of England, of what condition he be, free or bond, able in body, and within the age of sixty years . . . shall be bound to serve him which shall so require him; and take only the wages, livery, meed, or salary which were accustomed to be given.

War and Revolts

Despite all its threatened punishments, the Statute of Laborers, and similar measures elsewhere, were ineffective at stopping inflation. Instead they contributed to growing social resentment, which exploded in peasants' and workers' revolts. In France and England, these revolts were also sparked by a war between the two countries that had begun in 1337. The war had started over who would be the next French king and who would control certain parts of France, but eventually came to involve many other issues as well. It would later be given the name the Hundred Years' War, although it actually lasted even longer, from 1337 to 1453. The war devastated the French countryside; crops were stolen, villages were burned, and people and animals were killed.

The war caused taxes in France to go up dramatically, and after the plague swept through France there were fewer people left to pay them. In 1358, French peasants revolted against their landlords, many of whom were nobles who were exempted from paying taxes and who were losing to the English on the battlefield. Jean Froissart, a French historian and courtier generally favorable to the nobility, described these events in his chronicle written about a decade after they happened.

Some of the inhabitants of the country towns assembled together in Beauvoisis, without any leader: they were not at first more than one hundred men. They said, that the nobles of the kingdom of France, knights, and squires, were a disgrace to it, and that it would be a very meritorious act to destroy them all: to which proposition every one assented, as a truth, and added, shame befall him that should be the means of preventing the gentlemen from being wholly destroyed. They then, without further council, collected themselves in a body, and with no other arms than the staves shod with iron, which some had, and others with knives, marched on the house of a knight who lived near, and breaking it open, murdered the knight, his lady, and all the children, both great and small; they then burnt the house. . . .

They did the like to many castles and handsome houses and their numbers increased so much, that they were in a short time upwards of six thousand: wherever they went, they received additions, for all of their rank in life followed them, whilst every one else fled, carrying off with them their ladies, damsels, and children, ten or twenty leagues distant, where they thought they could place them in security, leaving their houses, with all their riches in them.

These wicked people, without leader and with arms, plundered and burnt all the houses they came to, murdered every gentleman, and violated every lady and damsel they could find. He who committed the most atrocious actions, and such as no human creature would have imagined, was the most applauded, and considered the greatest man among them. I dare not write the horrible and inconceivable atrocities they committed on the persons of the ladies . . . .

When the gentlemen of Beauvoisis, Corbie, Vermandois, and the lands where these wretches were associated, saw to what lengths their madness had extended, they sent for succour [help] to their friends in Flanders, Hainault, and Bohemia; from which places numbers soon came, and united themselves with the gentlemen of the country. They began therefore to kill and destroy these wretches wherever they met them, and hung them up by ropes on the nearest trees. The king of Navarre even destroyed in one day, near Clermont in Beauvoisis, upwards of three thousand: but they were by this time so much increased in number, that had they been altogether, they would have amounted to more than one hundred thousand. When they were asked for what reason they acted so wickedly; they replied, they knew not, but they did so because they saw others do it; and they thought by this means they should destroy all the nobles and gentlemen in the world.

Later in his chronicle, Froissart also reported on rebellion among the English peasants in 1381, where grievances centered on continuing labor obligations imposed by noble landlords. He described John Ball, a popular preacher, who both expressed and inspired social and religious grievances. In both France and England, the nobles were terrified at first, but they united against the peasants and hired trained, well-equipped soldiers to massacre groups of peasants armed only with hoes and bread knives. Reaction to revolts by workers seeking higher wages and better working conditions in cities such as Florence, Seville, and Lübeck was similarly brutal.

He was accustomed, every Sunday after mass, as the people were coming out of the church, to preach to them in the market place and assemble a crowd around him; to whom he would say,—"My good friends, things cannot go on well in England, nor ever will until every thing shall be in common; when there shall neither be vassal nor lord, and all distinctions leveled; when the lords shall be no more masters than ourselves. How ill have they used us! And for what reason do they thus hold us in bondage? Are we not all descended from the same parents, Adam and Eve? and what can they show or what reasons give, why they should be more the masters than ourselves? except, perhaps, in making us labour and work, for them to spend.

Writers such as Petrarch and Boccaccio lamented the tremendous loss of life, but they also used the tragedy as an inspiration for prose and poetry. Petrarch regarded his Latin scholarship as his most important work, but his hundreds of love poems, written to a mysterious woman named Laura, have been far more influential. Laura died in 1348 of the plague, but her death only inspired Petrarch to ever more beautiful sonnets in her praise.

> The eyes, the face, the limbs of heavenly mold,
> So long the theme of my impassioned lay,
> Charms which so stole me from myself away,
> That strange to other men the course I hold:

The crisped locks of pure and lucid gold,
The lightning of the angelic smile, whose ray
To earth could all of paradise convey,
A little dust are now, to feeling cold.

And yet I live!—but that I live bewail,
Sunk the loved light that through the tempest led
My shattered bark, bereft of mast and sail:

Hushed be the song that breathed love's purest fire!
Lost is the theme on which my fancy fed,
And turned to mourning my once tuneful lyre.

CHAPTER 2

The Past and the Perfect

In this fresco on the wall of the cathedral in Florence, the Italian writer Dante points toward sinners being led by demons to hell, one of the scenes from his most important work, *The Divine Comedy*, which he holds in his other hand. Behind the book rises the Florentine skyline, dominated by the cathedral with its eight-sided dome. When it was built, the cathedral was the largest Christian church in the world, a fitting symbol of Florence's prosperity.

The Renaissance began in the northern Italian city of Florence, which was situated on the fertile soil along the Arno River. The Roman emperor Julius Caesar founded the city in the first century B.C. as a home for army veterans, rewarding them with land after their long years of service in the Roman army. These veterans worked hard, as did the settlers who came after them, and the city flourished. Its favorable location on the main road northward from Rome made Florence a commercial hub, and the city grew wealthy buying and selling all types of goods throughout Europe and the Mediterranean—grain, cloth, wool, weapons, armor, spices, glass, and wine. Florentine merchants also loaned and invested money, and invented new ways to keep track of how their businesses were going. By the early fourteenth century, the city had about 80,000 people living in it, about twice the population of London at that time.

Renaissance means "rebirth," and the scholars, writers, and artists who created Renaissance culture looked back to the classical past for their models, particularly to the writers and leaders of ancient Rome. This did not mean that they ignored their own society, however. For most humanists, the best life was one of action and service to the community. They thought that education and training should emphasize practical skills such as public speaking and writing that would prepare young men for careers in Florence and the other expanding cities of Italy. If these careers brought wealth and success, so much the better. No one in the Renaissance denied the central importance of religion in human life or the existence of God, but God could be worshipped just

The Ciompi Revolt

Not everyone in Florence benefited equally from the city's expanding economy. Wool cloth was Florence's most important export, but the many people who sheared sheep, carded fleece, spun thread, and wove cloth were often badly paid by the merchants who controlled the wool trade. In 1378, a group of wool-carders (*Ciompi* in Italian) presented petitions calling for an improvement in working conditions, and then forcibly took over city hall. Although most wool workers could not read or write, one who could described the events:

> The *popolo* [common people] entered the palace.... They ascended the bell tower and placed there the emblem of the blacksmiths' guild, that is, the tongs. Then the banners of the other guilds, both great and small, were unfurled from the windows of the palace.... Those inside the palace threw out and burned ... every document which they found. And they remained there, all that day and night, in honor of God. Both rich and poor were there, each one to protect the standard of his guild.
>
> The next morning the *popolo* brought the standard of justice [the symbol of Florentine government] from the palace and they marched, all armed, to the Piazza della Signoria, shouting "Long live the *popolo minuto!*" ["little people"].... Then the *popolo* entered [the palace], taking with them the standard of justice ... and they entered all the rooms and they found many ropes which [the authorities] had bought to hang the poor people.... Several young men climbed the bell tower and rang the bells to signal the victory which they had won in seizing the palace, in God's honor. Then they decided to do everything necessary to fortify themselves and to liberate the *popolo minuto*.

The city government, controlled by the wool merchants, gave in to their demands, but about a month later sent an army against the *Ciompi* and reestablished the old system.

as well in the marketplace as the monastery. The talents God had given were to be developed to their fullest and displayed to the world, not hidden away.

Education was not simply a matter of schools or limited to one's childhood for Renaissance thinkers. They felt they were living in a new age, with new values, which people needed to be informed about and instructed in putting into practice throughout their lives. Humanist authors thus attempted to mold new types of people to fit this new world. They were especially concerned with setting out ideals for the upper classes who were politically and economically powerful, but their works eventually found a much larger audience among middle-class people in cities, especially those who hoped to rise in stature. These new ideas rarely filtered down to the majority of the population, however, who continued to live in small villages, make their living by farming, and learn about the world orally, not through reading. The Renaissance was thus largely an urban movement.

Along with celebrating the classical past, humanism emphasized the importance of the individual. Families, religious brotherhoods, neighborhoods, workers' organizations, and other groups continued to have meaning in people's lives, but Renaissance thinkers increasingly viewed these groups as springboards to far greater individual achievement. They were especially interested in individuals who had risen above their backgrounds to become brilliant, powerful, or unique. Such individuals had the admirable quality of virtù, which is not virtue as we use the word, but the ability to shape the world around them according to their will. Humanist historians included biographies of individuals with virtù in their histories of cities and nations, although they tended to focus on positive qualities, describing rulers and political leaders who were just, wise, pious, dignified, learned, brave, kind, and distinguished. For such flattering portraits of living rulers or their ancestors, authors sometimes received a position at court, or at least a substantial payment. The historian and political thinker Niccolò Machiavelli broke with this pattern, stating openly in The Prince that rulers who were most effective at shaping the world around them often relied on cunning and violence. He was not praised for his realism, however, but harshly criticized for not presenting an idealized view of political power.

Florence: A City of Gold

Nearly half the people of Florence died in the Black Death, but this did not destroy the city's prosperity. Those who remained alive were richer per capita, and thus better able to purchase luxury goods. In 1472, the Florentine merchant and historian Benedetto Dei boasted proudly of his city in

a letter to an acquaintance from Venice. Dei focused on the real gold that was found in Florence: gold coins stored in banks, gold thread woven into brocaded cloth, and gold wreaths worn by wealthy young women.

Florence is more beautiful and five hundred forty years older than your Venice. . . . We have round about us thirty thousand estates, owned by noblemen and merchants, citizens and craftsmen, yielding us yearly bread and meat, wine and oil, vegetables and cheese, hay and wood, to the value of nine hundred thousand ducats in cash, as you Venetians, Genoese, Chians, and Rhodians who come to buy them know well enough. We have two trades greater than any four of yours in Venice put together—the trades of wool and silk. Witness the Roman court and that of the King of Naples, the Marches and Sicily, Constantinople and Pera, Broussa and Adrianople, Salonika and Gallipoli, Chios and Rhodes, where, to your envy and disgust, in all of those places there are Florentine consuls and merchants, churches and houses, banks and offices, and whither go more Florentine wares of all kinds, especially silken stuffs and gold and silver brocades, than from Venice, Genoa, and Lucca put together. . . . Our beautiful Florence contains within the city in this present year two hundred seventy shops belonging to the wool merchants' guild, from whence their wares are sent to Rome and the Marches, Naples and Sicily, Constantinople and Pera, Adrianople, Broussa, and the whole of Turkey. It contains also eighty-three rich and splendid warehouses of the silk merchants' guild, and furnishes gold and silver stuffs, velvet, brocade, damask, taffeta, and satin. . . . The number of banks amounts to thirty-three; the shops of the cabinet-makers, whose business is carving and inlaid work, to eighty-four; and the workshops of the stonecutters and marble workers in the city and its immediate neighbourhood, to fifty-four. There are forty-four goldsmiths' and jewellers' shops, thirty gold-beaters, silver-wire-drawers, and a wax-figure maker. . . .

Go through all the cities of the world, nowhere will you ever be able to find artists in wax equal to those we now have in Florence. Another flourishing industry is the making of light and elegant gold and silver wreaths and garlands, which are worn by young maidens of high degree. Sixty-six is the number of the apothecaries' and grocer shops; seventy that of the butchers, besides eight large shops in which are sold fowl of all kinds.

Financially successful Florentines did not spend all of their money on luxurious clothing and jewelry, however, but also supported artists, musicians, and writers. These talented individuals represented a different sort

gold-beaters
Gold-beaters hammered gold into very thin sheets for artists and furniture makers to be used as goldleaf and inlay

silver-wire-drawers
Silver-wire-drawers spun silver and gold into thread to be used in elegant embroidery

I see the robbers, hangmen, freebooters and grooms of today more learned than the theologians and preachers of my day. What can I say? Even women and girls aspire to the honor and celestial manna of good learning. Things have changed so much that at my advanced age I have had to learn Greek.

—The learned giant Gargantua speaking to his son Pantagruel, in the satirical 1532 novel *Pantagruel* by French humanist author François Rabelais

of gold in which the city could take pride, as the humanist philosopher Marsilio Ficino wrote in a 1492 letter to a German friend. Ficino clearly felt that he was living in a golden age, when the arts and literature of the classical past had been restored to their former glory.

What the poets once sang of the four ages, lead, iron, silver, and gold, our Plato in the Republic transferred to the four talents of men, assigning to some talents a certain leaden quality implanted in them by nature, to others iron, to others silver, and to still others gold. If then we are to call any age golden, it is beyond doubt that age which brings forth golden talents in different places. That such is true of this our age he who wishes to consider the illustrious discoveries of this century will hardly doubt. For this century, like a golden age, has restored to light the liberal arts, which were almost extinct: grammar, poetry, rhetoric, painting, sculpture, architecture, music, the ancient singing of songs to the Orphic lyre, and all this in Florence. Achieving what had been honoured amoung the ancients, but almost forgotten since, the age has joined wisdom with eloquence, and prudence with the military art.

The Glories and Perils of Poetry

In the opinion of Ficino and other humanists, the ancient Roman author and statesman Cicero was the best example of the golden age of glory in language and literary style. Cicero had lived 1,500 years earlier, at the time of Julius Caesar, a turbulent era when Caesar and other powerful generals transformed the Roman republic into an empire. Many humanists saw this transformation as a betrayal, and the beginning of a long period of decay. In his history of Florence, written in 1436, the humanist historian and Florentine city official Leonardo Bruni closely linked the decline of Latin and the decline of the Roman republic.

The Latin language, in all its perfection and greatness, flourished most vigorously in the time of Cicero, for its first state was not polished or refined or subtle, but, mounting little by little to perfection, it reached its highest summit in the time of Cicero. After his age it began to sink and to descend, as until that time it had risen, and many years had not passed before it experienced a great decline and diminution; and it can be said that letters and the studies of the Latin language went hand in hand with the condition of the Roman Republic, which had also grown in power until the age of Cicero.

After the liberty of the Roman people had been lost through the rule of the emperors, who did not desist from killing and eliminating the men of excellence, the flourishing condition of studies and of letters perished, together with the welfare of the city of Rome . . .

As the city of Rome was destroyed by the emperors, who were perverse tyrants, so studies and Latin letters experienced a like ruin and decay, to such an extent that finally almost no one could be found who understood Latin literature with any refinement. Then Italy was invaded successively by the Goths and the Lombards, barbarian and foreign peoples, who almost completely extinguished all knowledge of letters.

In this same book, Bruni was also very clear that the period of decay had ended and a new era begun. He was the first to divide history into three eras—ancient, medieval, and modern—although another humanist historian actually invented the term "Middle Ages." Bruni had no doubts about who was responsible for the rebirth of classical glory and the beginning of the modern age: Petrarch.

A drawing of the Tempietto, or little temple, built in 1502 by the Florentine architect Donato Bramante for the pope in Rome. Bramante designed this as the ideal building; its basic shape is the circle, which was viewed as the most perfect form, and every part was proportioned according to classical standards. Unfortunately Bramante could not control what was built around it, and other buildings quickly crowded it.

Francesco Petrarch was the first who had such grace of talent, and who recognized and restored to light the ancient elegance of style which was lost and dead, and although in him it was not perfect, nevertheless by himself he saw and opened the way to this perfection, by recovering the works of Cicero, by enjoying them, by understanding them, and by adapting himself as much as he could, and he learned the way to that most elegant and perfect fluency. Certainly he did enough merely by showing the way to those who came after him. Thus, devoted to these studies and manifesting his talent even as a youth, Petrarch was much honoured and renowned. . . .

The honours of Petrarch were such that no man of his age was more highly esteemed than he, not only beyond the Alps but in Italy herself. For, coming to Rome, he was solemnly crowned poet laureate.

An aging Petrarch holds a copy of his book of sonnets in this illumination from a fifteenth-century manuscript copy of the book of sonnets itself. The artist places Petrarch inside the golden "V" that is the first letter in the book, and Petrarch's beloved Laura—forever youthful because she died in the plague—in a medallion within the intricate border.

In conclusion, so great was his fame and the honour accorded him by all cities and states and by all the people throughout Italy, that it seemed an incredible and wonderful thing.

Not everyone saw the honor accorded Petrarch and the rebirth of writing in the same positive way that Bruni did, however. Petrarch himself was skeptical, as he wrote in a letter to a friend in 1352, about a decade after he had been crowned poet laureate in Rome.

Is it then true that this disease of writing, like other malignant disorders, is, as the Satirist claims, incurable, and, as I begin to fear, contagious as well? How many, do you reckon, have caught it from me? Within our memory, it was rare enough for people to write verses. But now there is no one who does not write them; few indeed write anything else. . . . Our sons formerly employed themselves in preparing such papers as might be useful to themselves or their friends, relating to family affairs, business, or the wordy din of the courts. Now we are all engaged in the same occupation, and it is literally true, as Horace says, "learned or unlearned, we are all writing verses alike."

Petrarch may perhaps have been writing tongue-in-cheek when he describes poetry as a "disease," but he goes on in the letter to worry about how far the contagion has spread. Apparently nothing will please the crowds of people who ask for his opinion, one of the pressures of being a celebrity. Petrarch had doubts about fame, and spent the last years of his life in religious seclusion.

It is after all but a poor consolation to have companions in misery. I should prefer to be ill by myself. Now I am involved in others' ill-fortune as well as in my own, and am hardly given time to take a breath. For every day letters and poems from every corner of our land come showering down on my devoted head. Nor does this satisfy my foreign friends. I am overwhelmed by floods of missives, no longer from France alone, but from Greece, from Germany, from England. I am unable to judge even my own work, and yet I am called upon to be the universal critic of others. Were I to answer the requests in detail, I should be the busiest of mortals. If I condemn the composition, I am a jealous carper at the good work of others; if I say a good word for the thing, it is attributed to a mendacious desire to be agreeable; if I keep silence altogether, it is because I am rude, pert fellow. They are afraid, I infer, that my disease will not make away with me promptly enough. Between their goading and my own madness I shall doubtless gratify their wishes.

Fame and the Renaissance Man

Most Renaissance writers and artists were far less hesitant about the virtues of glory than Petrarch was, and praised individuals who showed *virtù*, that ability to shape the world around them. They did not exclude themselves when they searched for models of talent and achievement. Many Renaissance artists painted self-portraits, sometimes several dozen over the course of their lives. Humanist writers molded their own life stories into models for others. Leon Battista Alberti had much to be proud of: He wrote novels, plays, legal treatises, a study of the family, and the first scientific analysis of perspective; he designed churches, palaces, and fortifications effective against cannons; he invented codes for sending messages secretly and a machine that could cipher and decipher them. In his autobiography—written late in his life, and in the third person, so that he calls himself "he" instead of "I"—Alberti describes his personal qualities and accomplishments. His achievements in many fields did make Alberti into a "Renaissance man," although it might be hard to believe everything he said, especially his comments toward the end that "ambition was alien to him."

In everything suitable to one born free and educated liberally, he was so trained from boyhood that among the leading young men of his age he was considered by no means the last. For, assiduous in the science and skill of dealing with arms and horses and musical instruments, as well as in the pursuit of letters and the fine arts, he was devoted to the knowledge of the most strange and difficult things. And finally he embraced with zeal and forethought everything which pertained to fame. To omit the rest, he strove so hard to attain a name in modeling and painting that he wished to neglect nothing by which he might gain the approbation of good men. His genius was so versatile that you might almost judge all the fine arts to be his. Neither ease nor sloth held him back. . . .

He played ball, hurled the javelin, ran, leaped, wrestled, and above all delighted in the steep ascent of mountains; he applied himself to all these things for the sake of health rather than sport or pleasure. As a youth he excelled in warlike games. With his feet together, he could leap over the shoulders of men standing by; he had almost no equal among those hurling the lance. An arrow shot by his hand from his chest could pierce the strongest iron breastplate . . . . He learned music without teachers, and his compositions

In this fresco from the walls of an elegant rural house, stylishly dressed men with gloves and high boots prepare to go hunting with greyhounds, assisted by the short man in the middle who is most likely the servant who cared for the dogs. Hunting from horseback was one of the skills expected of a well-rounded Renaissance man.

were approved by learned musicians. Not a few musicians became more learned by virtue of his advice.

When he had begun to mature in years, neglecting everything else, he devoted himself entirely to the study of letters . . . . At the age of twenty-four he turned to physics and the mathematical arts . . . .

Although he was affable, gentle and harmful to no one, nevertheless he felt the animosity of many evil men, and hidden enmities, both annoying and very burdensome; in particular the harsh injuries and intolerable insults from his own relatives. . . . For they took it ill to be exceeded in ability and fame by him who, far inferior to them in fortune, had striven with such zeal and industry . . .

Among the Italian princes and among foreign kings, witnesses and heralds of his virtue were not lacking. He did not make use of their favour for any revenge, however, although he was continually disturbed by new injuries and could easily have avenged himself. When in the course of time, moreover, it came about that his private fortune was of great value to those by whom he had been gravely injured, he preferred to pay them back with kindness, benefits, and all kinds of philanthropy rather than to take revenge, so that the scoundrels regretted that they had injured such a man . . . .

He had within himself a ray by which he could sense the good or evil intentions of men towards himself. Simply by looking at them, he could discover most of the defects of anyone in his presence. . . . Ambition, however, was so alien to him that he even ascribed his own deeds, worthy of memory, to his elders in his book On the Family. And he also put in his own works the titles of others, and there exist whole works devoted to the fame of his friends.

Perfect Gentlemen, Perfect Ladies

Biographies and autobiographies presented individuals their authors thought were worthy models, but sometimes people needed more direct instruction. The ancient Greek philosopher Plato, whom Ficino mentioned in his praise of Florence, taught that the best way to learn something was to think about its perfect, ideal form. If you wanted to learn about justice, for example, you should imagine what ideal justice would be, rather than look at actual examples of justice in the world around you, for these would never be perfect. Following Plato's ideas, Renaissance authors speculated about perfect examples of many things. Alberti wrote about the ideal country house, which was to be useful, convenient, and elegant. The English humanist and official Thomas More described a perfect society, which he called Utopia, a word he invented that means "nowhere." Writers portrayed perfection in individuals as well, and their books often came to serve as how-to manuals for people seeking to improve themselves and rise in the social hierarchy. One of the most widely read of these was a book of manners for the perfect gentleman, written in the 1550s by the Italian poet and diplomat Giovanni della Casa and widely translated into many languages.

Although liberality, courage, or generosity are without doubt far greater and more praiseworthy things than charm and manners, none the less, pleasant habits and decorous manners and words are perhaps no less useful to those who have them than a noble spirit and self-assurance are to others. . . .

Let us say, then, that every act which is disgusting to the senses, unappealing to human desires, and also every act that brings to mind unpleasant matters or whatever the intellect finds disgusting, is unpleasant and ought to be avoided. Dirty, foul, repulsive or disgusting

Baldassar Castiglione looks calm and controlled, exactly like the ideal courtier he described, in this portrait by the renowned painter Raphael. His elegant but understated jacket and hat would have been perfect dress for a courtier, who was not supposed to be more noticeable than the ruler he served.

things are not to be done in the presence of others, nor should they even be mentioned. And not only is it unpleasant to do them or recall them, but it is also very bothersome to others even to bring them to mind with any kind of behaviour . . . .

And when you have blown your nose you should not open your handkerchief to look inside, as if pearls or rubies might have descended from your brain. This is a disgusting habit which is not apt to make anyone love you, but rather, if someone loved you already, he is likely to stop there and then. The spirit in the Labyrinth, whoever he may have been, proves this: in order to cool the ardour of Messer Giovanni Boccaccio for a lady he did not know very well, he tells Boccaccio how she squats over ashes and coughs and spits up huge globs.

It is also an unsuitable habit to put one's nose over someone else's glass of wine or food to smell it. By the same token I would not want someone to smell even his own drink or food for fear that some things that men find disgusting may drop from his nose, even if it should not happen.

When one speaks with someone, he should not get so close to the man that he breathes on his face, for you will find that many men do not like to smell someone else's breath, even though it may not have any bad odour to it.

In conversations, one can err in many various ways. First, the choice of topic should not be either frivolous or sordid, since listeners will not pay attention to such subjects nor take pleasure in them. On the contrary, they will despise both the discussions and the speaker. Also, one must not discuss subtle or arcane topics, for the majority of people can hardly understand them. Instead, one must diligently choose a topic so that no one in the group will be embarrassed or ashamed. Nor should anyone speak of filthy matters even if they were pleasant to hear, for honourable people should try to please others with honourable subjects . . . .

At a feast or at the table one should not tell sad stories, nor mention nor remind people of wounds, diseases, deaths, and plagues, or any other painful subject. And if anyone else lapses into this sort of conversation, one must gently and correctly change the subject and provide a happier and more suitable one.

Nor should a man boast of his nobility, his titles, his riches, least of all his intelligence. Nor should he praise at length, as some do, his past deeds and accomplishments, nor those of his ancestors, for in so doing it seems that he wants either to challenge those present who show themselves to be or who aspire to be equally as noble, as well off, and as capable, or to overwhelm them if they are of lesser stature, even appearing to chastise them for their humble origins and their poverty. In both cases such behaviour displeases everybody.

Therefore, a man must not be content with doing what is good, but he must also seek to do it gracefully.

Della Casa's manual was written only for men, but the diplomat Baldassar Castiglione included both gentlemen and ladies in *The Courtier*, a description of the type of courtiers that rulers would want to have surrounding them, written over several decades and published in 1528 just before Castiglione's death. *The Courtier* became a guide to proper behavior for nobles at court, and later for middle-class people with aspirations of rising in social status as well. Castiglione's advice for women has been particularly long-loved.

I think that in her ways, manners, words, gestures, and bearing, a woman ought to be very unlike a man; for just as he must show a certain solid and sturdy manliness, so it is seemly for a woman to have a soft and delicate tenderness, with an air of womanly sweetness in her every movement . . .

[Again] . . . many virtues of the mind are as necessary to a woman as to a man; also, gentle birth; to avoid affectation, to be naturally graceful in all her actions, to be mannerly, clever, prudent,

Stylish young Italian men and women play chess in this painting that once decorated the side of a wedding chest made to house a woman's *trousseau*. Properly educated gentlemen and ladies were expected to know how to play chess, although they were not to take it too seriously, but retain their sophistication and grace.

not arrogant, not envious, not slanderous, not vain, not contentious, not inept, to know how to gain and hold the favor of her mistress [queen or presiding lady at court] and of all others to perform well and gracefully the exercises that are suitable for women. And I do think that beauty is more necessary to her than to the Courtier, for truly that woman lacks much who lacks beauty. . . . For the sake of appearing free and amiable she must not utter unseemly words or enter into any immodest and unbridled familiarity or into ways such as might cause others to believe about her what is perhaps not true; but when she finds herself present at such talk, she ought to listen with a light blush of shame. . . .

And to repeat briefly a part of what has already been said. I wish this Lady to have knowledge of letters, of music, of painting, and know how to dance and how to be festive, adding a discreet modesty and the giving of a good impression of herself to those other things that have been required of the Courtier. And so, in her talk, in her laughter, her play, her jesting, in short in everything, she will be most graceful and will converse appropriately with every person in whose company she may happen to be, using witticism and pleasantries that are becoming to her.

A Perfect Prince or a Perfect Tyrant?

Ideal courtiers and court ladies should preferably serve an ideal ruler, and a number of Renaissance authors wrote works that set out ideals of government or described perfect political leaders. When his political career was ruined because a rival group gained power in Florence and he was banished, the Florentine government official and writer Niccolò Machiavelli first followed this pattern. He wrote several long works of history and political philosophy that describe Florence's republican form of government as ideal and portray its leaders positively. Machiavelli is best remembered not for these, however, but for his short work, *The Prince*, which sets out a much different ideal for rulers. Here Machiavelli asserts that the function of a ruler (or any government) is to preserve order and security. To do this the ruler should use whatever means he needs, including brutality, lying, and manipulation. Like the good humanist he was, Machiavelli presented examples from the classical past of just the type of ruler he was describing, as well as examples from the present. *The Prince* is often seen as the first modern guide to politics, though Machiavelli was later denounced for writing it, and people came to use the word "Machiavellian" to mean cunning and ruthless. Machiavelli did not say that rulers

Old Nick

Not only did Machiavelli's last name come to have a negative meaning, but his first name did as well, as people in England linked it with a traditional term for the Devil, "Old Nick." The poet Samuel Butler thought that this was unfair, and wrote in 1678 that many of Machiavelli's critics were hypocrites who claimed they were just and moral but actually treated people worse than a "Machiavellian" ruler would:

Nick Machiavel had ne'er a trick,
Tho' he gave his name to our old Nick.

can do anything they want, however, but that they should be judged on the results of their actions, not their personal qualities. He put a new spin on the Renaissance search for perfection, arguing that ideals needed to be measured in the cold light of the real world.

A prince should therefore have no other aim or thought, nor take up any other thing for his study, but war and its organization and discipline, for that is the only art that is necessary to one who commands, and it is of such virtue that it not only maintains those who are born princes, but often enables men of private fortune to attain to that rank. And one sees, on the other hand, that when princes think more of luxury than of arms, they lose their state. The chief cause of the loss of states is the contempt of this art, and the way to acquire them is to be well versed in the same. . . .

But as to exercise for the mind, the prince ought to read history and study the actions of eminent men, see how they acted in warfare, examine the causes of their victories and defeats in order to imitate the former and avoid the latter, and above all, do as some men have done in the past, who have imitated some one, who has been much praised and glorified, and have always kept his deeds and actions before them. . . .

It now remains to be seen what are the methods and rules for a prince as regards his subjects and friends. . . .

From this arises the question whether it is better to be loved more than feared, or feared more than loved. The reply is, that one ought to be both feared and loved, but as it is difficult for the two to go together, it is much safer to be feared than loved, if one of the two has to be wanting . . . Men have less scruple in offending one who makes himself loved than one who makes himself feared; for love is held by a chain of obligation which, men being selfish, is broken whenever it serves their purpose; but fear is maintained by a dread of punishment which never fails.

Still, a prince should make himself feared in such a way that if he does not gain love, he at any rate avoids hatred; for fear and the absence of hatred may well go together, and will be always attained by one who abstains from interfering with the property of his citizens and subjects or with their women. And when he is obligated to take the life of any one, let him do so when there is a proper justification and manifest reason for it; but above all he must abstain from taking the property of others, for men forget more easily the death of their father than the loss of their patrimony.

Niccolò Machiavelli gazes out of this portrait painted several decades after his death with lively eyes and a bemused smile, in seeming contrast to his tumultuous career. Although he was condemned in many parts of Europe after his death for his portrayal of the realities of political power, he was also celebrated in his home city of Florence and included in portrait galleries of important Florentines.

mit einem anderen puncten aber also piß das du die gantzen lauten gar an die tafel punctirst / dann
zeuch all puncten die auf der tafel von der lauten worden sind mit linien zůsamē / so sihst du was dar-
auß wirt / also magst du ander ding auch abzeychnen. Dise meynung hab ich hernach aufgeriffen.

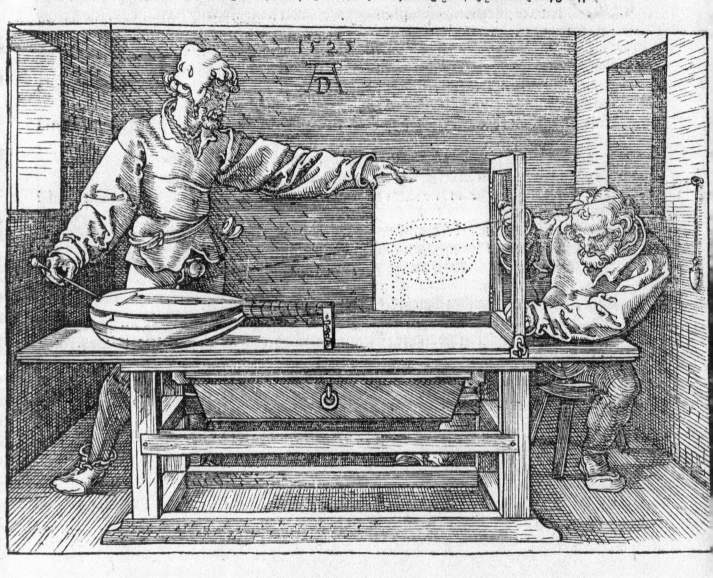

Vnd damit günstiger lieber Herr will ich meinem schreyben end geben / vnd so mir Got genad ver-
leycht die bücher so ich von menschlicher proporcion vn anderen darzů gehörend geschryben hab mit
der zeyt in druck pringen / vnd darpey meniglich gewarnet haben / ob sich yemand vnder-
steen wurd mir diß außgangen büchlein wider nach zů drucken / das ich das
selb auch wider drucken will / vn auß lassen geen mit meren vnd
grösserem zůsatz dañ ietz beschehen ist / darnach mag
sich ein yetlicher richtē / Got dem Herren
sey lob vnd eer ewigklich.

N iij

Gedruckt zů Núremberg.
Im. 1525. Jar.

CHAPTER 3

The Glory of the World

Humanists praised the wisdom of classical writers and philosophers, but some of them argued that the natural world, what they often called "the Book of Nature," was also a good teacher. Painters and sculptors agreed. They examined the natural world around them, seeking to understand how it worked and depict it more accurately. They experimented on practical problems such as perspective, that is, how to show three dimensions on a flat two-dimensional surface. They regarded everything as appropriate subject matter for their art, and did not draw a distinction between art and technology.

Leonardo da Vinci is the perfect example of the inquisitive Renaissance artist. Born in 1452 near Florence during the height of its prosperity, Leonardo wanted to reproduce what the eye can see, and he drew everything he saw around him, including executed criminals hanging on gallows as well as lovely women and the beauties of nature. Trying to understand how the human body worked, Leonardo studied live and dead bodies, doing autopsies and dissections to investigate muscles and the circulation of the blood. He carefully analyzed the effects of light, using his observations to paint strong contrasts of light and shadow. He was interested in the technical aspects of art, and tried new materials for painting and sculpture, some of which worked, and some of which did not. His painting of the Last Supper shows powerful human expressions in a way that influenced many later artists, but the painting itself began to flake off the wall as soon as it was finished, and has had to be restored many times. A gigantic bronze horse, for which he experimented with different techniques of casting and mixtures of

The German artist Albrecht Dürer shows two fellow artists using a mechanical apparatus to draw a lute accurately, and provides directions above about how to use it. Like many Renaissance artists, Dürer was fascinated with the theoretical and practical problems of perspective, and designed devices that could assist artists in solving these.

metals, was never finished. The bronze was eventually used for cannon in one of the many wars in Renaissance Italy. Many of Leonardo's ideas, such as the helicopter, tank, machine gun, and parachute, remained only sketches in his notebooks, as the materials that would allow them to become realities were only developed centuries later. Most of his writings are also in his notebooks, which were never published in his lifetime and are now scattered in many museums and libraries.

The drawings, paintings, and sculptures of many Renaissance artists, including Leonardo, present plants, animals, and other natural objects as accurately as possible. In such works, the aim of the artist was to reproduce nature, but there were others who thought that human intervention could improve on nature. The debate over the relative value of nature and "art"—by which people meant all types of human activity—was a common one in the Renaissance. It drew in scientists as well as artists, who invented various tools through which people could apply their ingenuity to explore nature more fully, including magnifying lenses and the telescope.

Whereas artists and scientists closely studied the human body as part of nature, poets, playwrights, and philosophers turned their attention to the human spirit, will, and emotions. They debated whether there were limits to what people could accomplish, and explored the heights and depths of human feelings in poems, plays, stories, and treatises.

Composers and musicians also expressed the emotions in songs, hymns, and instrumental music. Classical philosophers such as Plato had justified music by pointing out the relationship between musical harmony and other harmonies in the universe, but there was no way for anyone to know how Roman and Greek music had sounded, so it could not be used as a model. This did not keep people from playing many types of music. Nobles and church officials hired professional musicians and composers, both for special occasions like weddings or processions and as permanent staff. Plays included music, fairs and inns provided a place to both listen and perform, village families sometimes sang as they worked, and wealthier urban and aristocratic families sang or played instruments together, including recorders, shawms (a type of oboe), sackbuts (trombones), and various types of string instruments.

This study of the world and the role of humans in it was a celebration as well as a task, for most Renaissance thinkers agreed that the material world was something to be enjoyed and praised. Earthly beauty was created by God, and so was a reflection of divine beauty. The material world might be imperfect—love could cause great pain, beauty was often fleeting, people were capable of horrific cruelty—but it also contained wonders.

The Book of Nature

One of the strongest arguments that God's work could be seen directly in nature came from Bernard Palissy (1510–1590), a self-taught French potter, glass painter, and natural scientist. (We would probably call him a geologist, but study of the natural world was not divided into specialties in the Renaissance as it is today.) Palissy wandered the hills around his home, observing the action of wind and rain, and speculated that these caused the erosion of mountains and the creation of soil. He found fossils, some of which were plants and animals he did not recognize, and suggested that these were the remains of species that had become extinct. He used plants and dead animals, especially small snakes, lizards, shells, and fish, to make molds, and attached the figures that came out of the molds to ceramic platters designed to re-create their natural setting as closely as possible. Colors and surface textures were also to mimic those of nature, and Palissy experimented with dyes and glazes made from metals, salts, and clays. When he was in his sixties, he gave a series of lectures on natural history in Paris, and later collected them in *Admirable Discourses*, published in 1580. He dedicated the book to a French nobleman who had been his patron and friend, explaining his motivation in the opening section.

It is written one should take care not to abuse the gifts of God and hide one's talent in the earth; and also that the fool who hides his folly is worth more than the wise man who conceals his wisdom. It is therefore, just and reasonable that each one should seek to multiply the talents he has received from God, following His commandment. For this reason I have striven to bring to light the things it has pleased God to make me understand, according to the measure with which it has pleased him to endow me, in order to benefit posterity. And it seems that many in fine Latin or some other well-polished language have left many pernicious talents to harm the young and waste their time . . . . Such harmful books have induced me to scrape the earth for forty years and to dig into its entrails in order to know the things it produces within itself, and in this way I have found grace before God, who has enabled me to know secrets heretofore unknown to men, even to the most learned, as one can know from my writings contained in this book.

I know well that some will make fun of me, saying it is impossible that a man deprived of the Latin language could attain an understanding of natural things; and they will say that I have great temerity in writing against the opinion of so many famous and ancient philosophers, who have written about natural effects

The Body and Its Secrets

The Flemish physician Andreas Vesalius asserted that the inside of the human body should be just as open to study as the inside of the earth, and carried out dissections on cadavers while his students crowded around. He was criticized by other doctors, who rarely touched a patient, much less a dead body, because university medical training at that time centered on mastery of key ancient texts such as those of Aristotle, and regarded hands-on learning as inferior. In the introduction to his major work on anatomy, *On the Structure of the Human Body* (1543), Vesalius commented that such ideas should be "despised . . . as the fundamental nature and rational basis of the art of medicine prescribes that the hand should also be applied to the treatment, lest such physicians slash the body of medicine and make of it a force destructive of the common life of man."

In this earthenware platter, Bernard Palissy gives the impression of looking down through a stream to the mud and stones below. The slithering snake and other small animals were cast from real specimens, with the ripples and other details carefully carved before the platter was fired in a kiln.

and filled all this earth with wisdom. I know also that some will judge by appearances, saying that I am only a poor artisan, and by such talk will try to discredit my writings. In truth there are things in my book which it will be difficult for the ignorant to believe. Despite all these considerations, I have persisted in my enterprise, and in order to cut short all kinds of calumnies and attacks, I have made up a collection in which I have put many admirable and wonderful things that I have drawn from the matrix of the earth, which serve as certain proof of what I say.

Nature versus Art

The debate about the value of "nature" created by God and "art" created by human beings involved not only artists, but also writers and philosophers. In one of his last plays, *The Winter's Tale,* written around 1610, William Shakespeare puts this debate into the mouths of two characters, King Polixenes of Bohemia and Perdita, the daughter of the King of Sicily. In the kind of complicated plot twist so common in Shakespeare, Perdita had been abandoned as an infant when her jealous father thought that Polixenes was her real father, but was found by a shepherd and raised as his own daughter. She knows nothing of her real identity. Polixenes's son (dressed in simple clothes to conceal his true identity) has fallen in love with her, and his father (wearing a disguise so his own son does not recognize him) comes to intervene. Perdita is gathering flowers, and Polixenes asks her for some. It is early April, before most flowers have bloomed, and she apologizes that she has few of the streaked carnations and gillyvors that grow best in winter. She explains her reasons for not planting them, and Polixenes responds with a defense of the "art"—in this case artificial cross-breeding or grafting—that produces streaked flowers. Artificial breeding works *through* nature, he argues, not against it, and improves plants and animals by adding "nobler" qualities.

At this point in the play, all of the main characters are dressed as something they are not. In other words, they, too, are all "artificial," but only we as the audience know all the complications. So what might seem to be a simple debate about flower-breeding is actually a debate about whether human actions improve or distort nature, with the debaters taking positions they don't really represent. Perdita argues against cross-breeding, but she is herself a princess who thinks she is a shepherd's daughter. (And she's actually dressed as the queen of an upcoming spring festival, so there is *another* layer to her identity in this scene.) Polixenes defends cross-breeding as a gift of nature, but later in this scene is horrified when his son wants to marry Perdita. Adding "nobler" qualities by cross-breeding was fine for plants and animals, but not for humans, and especially not for his son. He accuses Perdita of bewitching his son, threatens to "scratch her beauty with briers," and to disinherit his son and kill her if they ever see each other again. Shakespeare wrote *The Winter's Tale* as a comedy, so there is a happy ending once everyone's true identity is revealed. The play does not resolve the art versus nature debate, but, like all of Shakespeare's plays, shows life to be more complicated than it seems.

Polixenes: Shepherdess,
    A fair one are you. Well you fit our ages
    With flowers of winter.
Perdita: Sir, the year growing ancient
    Not yet on summer's death, nor on the birth
    Of trembling winter, the fairest flowers o'th' season
    Are our carnations and streaked gillyvors,
    Which some call nature's bastards. Of that kind
    Our rustic garden's barren, and I care not
    To get slips of them.
Polixenes: Wherefore, gentle maiden,
    Do you neglect them?
Perdita: For I have heard it said

> **Piedness**
> Streaked color

    There is an art which in their piedness shares
    With great creating nature.
Polixenes: Say there be,
    Yet nature is made better by no mean
    But nature makes that mean. So over that art
    Which you say adds to nature is an art
    That nature makes. You see, sweet maid, we marry
    A gentler scion to the wildest stock,
    And make conceive a bark of baser kind
    By bud of nobler race. This is an art
    Which does not mend nature—change it rather; but
    The art itself is nature
Perdita: So it is.
Polixenes: Then make your garden rich in gillyvors,
    And do not call them bastards.
Perdita: I'll not put

> **Dibble**
> Trowel

    The dibble in earth to set one slip of them.

Shakespeare's Ironies

Much of what makes Shakespeare's plays so interesting even four hundred years after they were written is his sense of the irony of the human condition, and his ability never to let the audience know exactly what he is thinking. These come out in *The Winter's Tale*, and even more in his most famous play, *Hamlet, the Prince of Denmark*, written in 1600. Shakespeare has Hamlet proclaim, "What a piece of work is a man! How noble in reason! How infinite in faculty! In form, in moving, how express and admirable! In action how like an angel! In apprehension how like a god!" These lines echo the words written a century earlier by the Italian humanist Pico della Mirandola, whose "Oration on the Dignity of Man" included similar statements: "Man is the most fortunate and worthy of creatures . . . man is rightly called and considered a great miracle and a truly marvelous creature . . . . Whatever seeds each man cultivates will grow and bear fruit in him . . . if they are rational, he will become like a heavenly creature; if intellectual, he will be an angel and a son of God." Hamlet's ringing speech occurs in a scene where people are trying to figure out whether he is insane or just pretending to be, whereas Pico's oration was an introduction to nine hundred philosophical theses he had determined were true and wanted to defend. So are Hamlet's words a sign of his insanity or his intelligence? Did Shakespeare agree with these ideas, or was he mocking them? Millions of readers, theatre-goers, and movie viewers have debated these questions, and many others that the play leaves open.

Painters, Poets, and Nature

Whereas Shakespeare encourages his audience to think about the merits of nature as compared to "art," other people debated the value of different types of creative activity. Leonardo was one of these, and in one of the reflections recorded in his notebooks, he makes his opinion about the merits of painting when compared to poetry or other types of writing very clear.

Painting is born of nature—or, to speak more correctly, we will say it is the grandchild of nature; for all visible things are produced by nature, and these her children have given birth to painting. Hence we may justly call it the grandchild of nature and related to god.

The eye, which is called the window of the soul, is the principal means by which the central sense can most completely and abundantly appreciate the infinite works of nature; and the ear is the second, which acquires dignity by hearing of the things the eye has seen. If you, historians or poets or mathematicians, had not seen things with your eyes you could not report of them in writing. And if you, O poet, tell a story with your pen, the painter with his brush can tell it more easily, with simpler completeness and less tedious to be understood. And if you call painting dumb poetry, the painter may call poetry blind painting. Now which is the worse defect? to be blind or dumb? Though the poet is as free as the painter in the invention of his fictions, they are not so satisfactory to men as paintings; for though poetry is able to describe forms, actions, and places in words, the painter deals with the actual similitude of the forms, in order to represent them. Now tell me which is the nearer to the actual man: the name of man or the image of man? The name of man differs in different countries, but his form is never changed but by death.

And if the poet gratifies the sense by means of the ear, the painter does so by the eye—the worthier sense; but I will say no more of this but that, if a good painter represents the fury of a battle, and if a poet describes one, and they are both together put before the public, you will see where most of the spectators will stop, to bestow most praise, and which will satisfy them best. Undoubtedly painting, being by a long way the more intelligible and beautiful, will please most. Write up the name of God [Christ] in some spot and set up His image opposite and see which will be most reverenced. Painting comprehends in itself all the forms of nature, while you have nothing but words, which are not universal, as form is, and if you have the effects of representation, we have the representation of the effects. Take a poet who describes the beauty of a lady to her lover and a painter who represents her and you will see to which nature guides the enamoured critic, . . . we, by our arts, may be called the grandsons of God. If poetry deals with moral philosophy, painting deals with natural philosophy. Poetry describes the actions of the mind, painting considers what the mind may effect by the motions [of the body]. If poetry can terrify people by hideous fictions, painting can do as much by depicting the same things in action. Suppose that a poet applies himself to represent beauty, ferocity, or a base, a foul, or a monstrous thing, as against a painter. He may in his ways bring forth a variety of forms; but will the painter not satisfy more? Are there not pictures to be seen, so like the actual things, that they deceive men and animals?

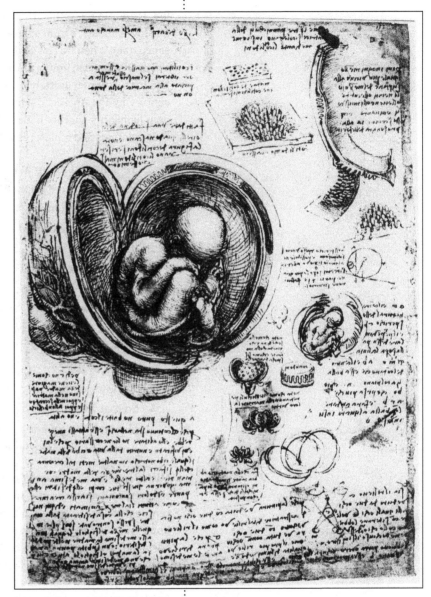

Leonardo da Vinci's drawing of a fetus in the womb, along with discussions and other sketches of fetal positions and the placenta, appears on one of the many thousands of pages of his notebooks. Leonardo drew and wrote about the world around him nearly every day, bringing together art and science.

The Artist as Poet

For Leonardo, painting was clearly superior to poetry, but other Renaissance artists did both. The biography of Michelangelo Buonarotti is the longest in *Lives of the Most Excellent Painters, Sculptors, and Architects*, with the art historian Giorgio Vasari describing him as a "genius universal in each art," by which Vasari meant painting, sculpture, and architecture. Michelangelo had been sent by "the great ruler in heaven . . . so that the world should marvel at the singular eminence of his life, work, and all his actions, seeming rather divine than earthly." Michelangelo was also a poet, writing verses first as a young man while at the court of Lorenzo de Medici, the ruler of his hometown of Florence, and then throughout his life. He wrote more than three hundred poems, including religious lyrics and love sonnets, a form of poetry that had been invented in early Renaissance Italy. When he was about sixty, he met the poet and noble widow Vittoria Colonna in Rome, and wrote some of his most effective poems for her. In this sonnet, written in about 1540 and translated in the nineteenth century by the American poet Henry Wadsworth Longfellow, Michelangelo highlights another issue in the debate over nature and art, the fact that paintings and sculptures will last long after their subjects have died.

> To Vittoria Colonna
> Lady, how can it chance—yet this we see
> In long experience—that will longer last
> A living image carved from quarries vast
> than its own maker, who dies presently?
> Cause yieldeth to effect if this so be,
> And even Nature is by Art surpassed;
> This know I, who to Art have given the past,
> But see that Time is breaking faith with me.
> Perhaps on both of us long life can I
> Either in color or in stone bestow,
> By now portraying each in look and mien;
> So that a thousand years after we die,
> How fair thou wast, and I how full of woe,
> And wherefore I so loved thee, may be seen.

Michelangelo also gave Colonna several drawings with religious themes, and at about the same time she gave him a small handwritten book of about a hundred spiritual sonnets she had composed. The book was crafted in the beautiful handwriting of her professional calligrapher, and became one of Michelangelo's most treasured possessions. In one of the book's last sonnets, Colonna mentions a tool that Michelangelo would be very familiar with—the file used to smooth and finish statues—as she describes the spark of divine inspiration that inspired her poetry.

> If I often fail to take up the file
> of good sense and, looking around me
> with scornful eyes, refuse to embellish
> or erase my rough uncultivated verses,
>   this is because my primary concern is not
> to garner praise for it, or avoid contempt,
> or that, after my joyful return to heaven,
> my poems will live on in the world more highly honored,

In this letter to Vittoria Colonna written in 1541, Michelangelo includes one of the many poems that he wrote for her. Learned men and women often wrote poetry for one another to demonstrate their esteem, admiration, and friendship; to show off their learning; or to flatter a possible patron.

but the divine fire, which through its mercy
inflames my mind, sometimes gives out
these sparks of its own accord,
     and if one such spark should once warm
some gentle heart, then a thousand times
a thousand thanks I owe to that happy mistake.

Fleeting Life, Fleeting Love

In his poem to Vittoria Colonna, Michelangelo warned he was to "die presently," and at sixty he was clearly old by Renaissance standards, though he actually lived to be almost ninety. The fleetingness of life was not only a concern of older people, however, but a common theme in Renaissance literature. Love poetry especially urges lovers to grab the moment. While the relationship between Vittoria Colonna and Michelangelo seems to have been a deep personal and spiritual friendship rather than a romantic attraction, most poetry celebrates earthly as well as divine love. The French lyric poet Pierre du Ronsard penned many verses noting how swiftly life was going by and how often love passed quickly as well. His poetry answered Leonardo's and Michelangelo's assertions about the value and permanence of painting and sculpture by stressing that poetry, too, could live beyond death, as in these two poems.

GATHER ROSE-BUDS
While this green month is fleeting,
Oh! come, my pretty sweeting,
   Waste not in the vain thy ring-time!
Sly age, ere we've an inkling
Thereof, our hair is sprinkling-
   He passeth even as Spring-time.
Then, while our life is crying
For love, and Time is flying,
   Come, love, come reap desire.
Pass love from vein to vein!
Swift comes old Death—and then
   All joys expire.

LIFE'S ROSES
When you are very old, by the hearth's glare,
   At candle-time, spinning and winding thread,
   You'll sing my lines, and say astonishéd:
Ronsard made these for me, when I was fair.

Then not a servant even, with toil and care
   Almost out-worn, hearing what you have said,
   Shall fail to start awake and lift her head
And bless your name with deathless praise fore'er.

My bones shall lie in earth, and my poor ghost
   Take its long rest where Love's dark myrtles thrive.
   You, crouching by the fire, old, shrunken, grey,

Shall rue your proud disdain and my love lost . . .
    Nay, hear me, love! Wait not to-morrow! Live,
And pluck life's roses, oh! to-day, to-day.

Most writers whose works were well-known in the Renaissance were men, and the small number of women who wrote tended to focus on religious or spiritual issues. One of the few women who wrote about romantic love was the well-educated, middle-class French woman Louise Labé, whose poems were published in a small volume in 1555. Her poetry about the heights and depths of love could be as powerful as that of her contemporary Ronsard, whose work she admired.

No wisdom of Ulysses could foresee
The woe and the disquiet that are mine
From looking on that countenance divine,
So full of honour, charm, and dignity.

Two radiant eyes have hurt me grievously,
Wounding my heart. And, Love, the fault is thine;
While thou, the fountain of heart's warmth and wine,
Alone can furnish it the remedy.

O cruel fate that from a Scorpion sting
Requires that I must suffer and entreat
The animal an antidote to bring!

End this my torment, but extinguish not
The need of love in me, that is so sweet
I could no longer live with love forgot.

LOISE LABBE LIONNOISE

In an engraving made at the time her poetry was first published, the French poet Louise Labé appears serene and respectable. Her poetry was dramatic and emotional, but questions about whether it was proper for women to write at all might have prompted her or her publisher to favor this rather demure portrayal.

Music to Charm the Soul

Painting, plays, and poetry offered ways to explore human emotions and the natural world, and so did music. The Italian diplomat Baldassar Castiglione, challenged as to whether music was an appropriate activity for men, defended it in *The Courtier*, his description of the ideal court gentleman and lady published in 1528.

You must think I am not pleased with the Courtier if he be not also a musician, and besides his understanding and cunning upon the book, have skill in the like manner on sundry instruments. For if we weigh it well, there is no ease of the labours and medicines of feeble minds to be found more honest and more praiseworthy in time of leisure than it . . . .

This fifteenth-century French manuscript of a love ballad was designed to be beautiful, but also useful to the singers, with a staff indicating the pitch of the notes and the notes themselves written in different forms indicating their length. Medieval monks invented the scale (including the do-re-mi-fa-so-la names for the note pitches) and musical notation to sing religious chants, and Renaissance composers developed these further.

I shall enter into a large sea of the praise of music and call to rehearsal how much it has always been renowned among them of old time and counted a holy matter; and how it has been the opinion of most wise philosophers that the world is made of music, and the heavens in their moving make a melody, and our soul framed after the very same sort, and therefore lifts up itself and (as it were) revives the virtues and force of itself with music . . . .

Do you not then deprive our Courtier of music, which does not only make sweet the minds of men, but also many times wild beasts tame.

As in all of his activities, however, a gentleman was not to show off or brag about his musical skills, as Castiglione made clear later in the same book.

Let our Courtier come to show his music as a thing to pass the time with, and as he were forced to do it, and not in the presence of noblemen, nor of any great multitude. And for all he be so skilful and does well understand it, yet will I have him to dissemble the study and pains that a man must needs take in all things that are well done. And let him make a semblance that he esteems but little in himself that quality, but in doing it excellently well, make it much esteemed of other men.

Both singing and playing instruments were appropriate for a courtier, and one instrument merited special praise from Castiglione.

[Singing] is a fair music, so it be done upon the book surely and after a good sort. But to sing to the lute is much better, because all the sweetness consists in one alone, and a man is much more heedful and understands better the feat manner and the air or vein of it when the ears are not busied in hearing any more than one voice; . . . singing to the lute . . . is more pleasant than the rest, for it adds to the words such a grace and strength that it is a great wonder.

Messages from the Stars

Lutes and recorders were not the only sorts of instruments that could help explore the place of humans in the world. The Italian scientist Galileo Galilei, whose father Vincenzo was a musical theorist, praised a different type of newly invented instrument, the telescope, in his *Starry Messenger*, published in 1610. Here Galileo excitedly reports his discovery of the four moons of Jupiter, which he named "Cosimo's stars" in honor of Grand Duke Cosimo de Medici, the ruler of Florence and his patron, to whom he sent a fancy copy of the book and a telescope as a gift. To Galileo, the fact there were heavenly bodies orbiting something other than the earth demonstrated that the traditional earth-centered view of the universe was wrong. Jupiter's moons supported the sun-centered theory first advanced by the Polish astronomer and scholar Nicolaus Copernicus in 1543, an idea that was still very controversial in the early seventeenth century. Galileo's call for "other discoveries, still more excellent," sounds much like Hamlet's comment that man is "infinite in faculty," although it seems to be said with enthusiasm rather than irony.

About ten months ago a report reached my ears that a Dutchman had constructed a telescope, by the aid of which visible objects, although at a great distance from the eye of the observer, were seen distinctly as if near; and some proofs of its most wonderful performances were reported. [This] determined me to give myself up first to inquire into the principle of the telescope, and then to consider the means by which I might compass the invention of a similar instrument . . . . At length, by sparing neither labour nor

Lutes were recommended as perfect instruments for women as well as men, for they allowed one to sing at the same time, and could be played alone or in a group. Good music played on the lute seemed able to reflect and express human emotion, as Louise Labé commented in one of her sonnets, published in 1555.

O lute, true friend in my adversity,
You witness first hand all my tears and moans.
You bring diversion when I'm woebegone,
And when I lose at love, you mourn with me.
Then, as I weep and strum a melody
At once, you render it in somber tones,
Transposing major keys to minor ones.
Dear friend, we work in perfect harmony.
And when I mingle pleasure with a sigh,
At once, you then switch back to major keys.
You know my moods so well that we become
As one. We're playing songs that satisfy,
Without constraint or dreary tedium,
And always with an ending bittersweet.

An elegant gentleman plays the lute and beautifully dressed ladies play the recorder, spinet (an ancestor of the piano), and viola da gamba (an early version of the cello). The artist puts the musicians in an idyllic outdoor setting to emphasize the way that music, like art, fit with the natural world.

In a series of sketches drawn on the back of an envelope, Galileo shows the movements of Jupiter's moons during the period January 14 to 25, 1611. Galileo saw these through an instrument with several lenses that had just been invented by Dutch spectacle-makers, and that he had improved. He called this new invention a perspecillum, but a mathematician friend soon gave it the name we use today: telescope, from the Greek words for "see" and "far."

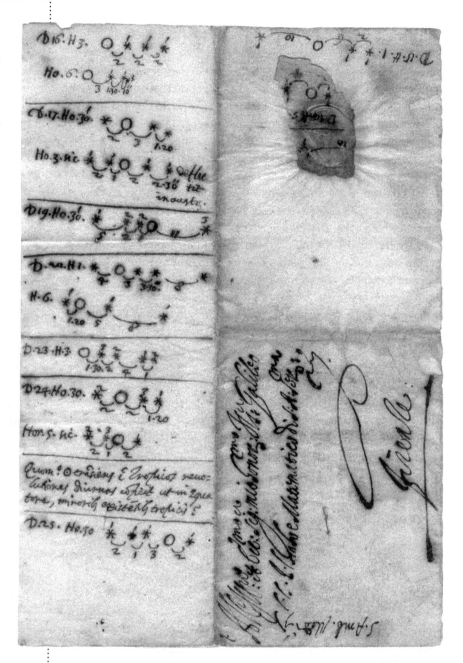

expense, I succeeded in constructing for myself an instrument so superior that objects seen through it appear magnified nearly a thousand times, and more than thirty times nearer than if viewed by the natural powers of sight alone.

First Telescopic Observations. It would be altogether a waste of time to enumerate the number and importance of the benefits which this instrument may be expected to confer, when used by land or sea. But without paying attention to its use for terrestrial objects, I betook myself to observations of the heavenly bodies; and first of all I viewed the moon as near as if it were scarcely two semidiameters of the earth distant. After the moon, I frequently observed other heavenly bodies both fixed stars and planets, with incredible delight . . .

But that which will excite the greatest astonishment by far, and which indeed especially moved me to call the attention of all astronomers and philosophers, is this: namely, that I have discovered four planets, neither known nor observed by any one of the astronomers before my time, which have their orbits round a certain bright star, one of those previously known, like Venus and Mercury round the sun, and are sometimes in front of it, sometimes behind it, though they never depart from beyond certain limits. All which facts were discovered and observed a few days ago by the help of a telescope devised by me, through God's grace first enlightening my mind.

Perchance, other discoveries still more excellent will be made from time to time by me or by other observers, with the assistance of a similar instrument.

The Individual and the Family

A goldsmith consults with a wealthy couple about a wedding ring, while some of his other products are displayed on the shelf behind, in this fifteenth-century oil painting by the Flemish artist Petrus Christus. The goldsmith's face is quite distinctive, while theirs are more generic, suggesting this is a portrait of a specific goldsmith.

Renaissance thinkers and writers celebrated people who had achieved greatness through their own talents and skills. Later historians saw this championing of the individual as a defining feature of Renaissance culture, separating it from the Middle Ages in which people had been thought of, and thought of themselves, primarily as part of a group. Art provides much evidence of this new individualism. Painters and sculptors began to sign their works, marking them as creations of a single person whose name was to be known and remembered. The subject matter of art changed as well. Along with biblical and historical scenes, artists were commissioned to paint increasing numbers of individual portraits, showing wealthy and powerful people with sumptuous clothing and furnishings. Some of these portraits were integrated into larger scenes with many figures, but many were stand-alone, with the sitter often looking directly out at the viewer, meeting the gaze of anyone who saw the painting. Along with portraits of others, many artists also painted self-portraits, sometimes a number of times during their lives. In both portraits and self-portraits, artists tried to capture their subjects' character and personality as well as physical appearance.

Along with the portraits of individuals that poured out of the studios of Renaissance artists, there were also many paintings that showed members of families together—married couples, fathers and sons, occasionally mothers and sons, uncles and nephews, and sometimes whole family groups. Such artistic evidence supports what written evidence has demonstrated: Despite the attention to individual achievement, people's identity remained firmly rooted in their families. This was particularly true for the nobility and for the broad mass of common people, but even among the Italian urban intellectuals who thought of themselves as living in a new era, family remained central to their understanding of themselves and their place in the world.

Domenico Ghirlandaio, *Confirmation of the Rule from the Sassetti Chapel,* 1483–1486

This fresco was one of six depicting events from the life of St. Francis commissioned by the Florentine banker Francesco Sassetti and painted by Domenico Ghirlandaio, whose apprentices included Michelangelo. In the foreground of the central scene showing the thirteenth-century saint receiving approval for his new religious order from the pope, Ghirlandaio added portraits of many prominent people in the Florence of his own day. To the right are Sassetti himself (bald and in a red robe), along with a black-haired Lorenzo de Medici, the most powerful man in Florence. Sassetti points to his three grown sons shown on the left, and Lorenzo watches his own younger sons come up the stairs with their tutor, the scholar Angelo Poliziano, followed by other humanists. The painting shows each of these people as distinct individuals, not as generic types, and affirms the connections of male members of the family to one another and to the new humanist learning.

Domenico Ghirlandaio, *An Old Man and His Grandson,* circa 1490

Some Renaissance portraits, especially those of women, were idealized, but many show their subjects with facial and bodily features that were not especially flattering, or with the wrinkles and thinning hair that come with age. In this portrait of a grandfather and his grandson, painted in tempera paint on wood, Ghirlandaio shows the older man with a nose covered in skin growths, but also holding the young child with great tenderness. Both the realistic portraiture and the depiction of family sentiment were qualities that distinguished Renaissance paintings from those produced in earlier centuries.

Michelangelo Buonoratti, *Pietà*, 1498

Michelangelo carved this exquisite statue of the Virgin Mary holding the dead body of her son Jesus when he was twenty-four, and had recently arrived in Rome from Florence. Across Mary's chest is a sash on which Michelangelo carved, in Latin, "Michelangelo Buonoratti of Florence was making this." In the inscription, he actually divided his first name into two parts—Michael Angelus—linking himself with Michael the Archangel, God's messenger. This is the only time that Michelangelo signed his name on an artwork, but the placement of the signature right across Mary's body, and his reference to the angels, suggests that Michelangelo himself thought his talents had divine origin. Later biographers and art historians would agree.

Albrecht Dürer, *Self-Portrait at Thirteen*, 1484

In this self-portrait, done using a silver-tipped pencil on specially prepared paper, the young Albrecht Dürer shows himself as a calm and composed adolescent. The inscription in German, written later by the artist, reads: "This I drew, using a mirror; it is my own likeness, in the year 1484, when I was still a child." Dürer was born to a goldsmith father in Nuremberg, a prosperous city in central Germany, and showed a talent for drawing early. He trained with various German artists, and traveled twice to Italy, studying with artists in Venice, where there was a large community of German merchants, and in other cities as well. This is the earliest of many self-portraits that Dürer drew and painted, each of which shows him in a different social role.

Albrecht Dürer, *Self-Portrait at Twenty-Six*, 1498

In this self-portrait, painted after he returned from his first trip to Italy, Dürer shows himself as a cosmopolitan dandy, with a fashionable tunic and cape, stylish hat, and expensive doeskin gloves. His clothing is fancier and more elaborate than that worn by the wealthier and more prominent residents of Nuremberg who commissioned most of his paintings. The inscription in German, reads: "I painted this from my own appearance; I was twenty-six years old." In its arrangement and style, it is modeled on Italian paintings, with soft coloring and a landscape out the window that looks more like Italian hills than the flat plain around Nuremberg. The portrait also conveys new ideas about the individual genius and high status of the artist that Dürer could have absorbed in Italy. On his second trip to Italy several years after this portrait was painted, he remarked directly on the contrast between the social prominence of artists in Italy and Germany, writing to a friend in Nuremberg, "Here I am a gentleman, at home only a parasite."

Albrecht Dürer, *Self-Portrait at Twenty-Eight*, 1500

In his last surviving painted self-portrait, Dürer shows himself staring directly out from the middle of the frame with hair that blends with his expensive fur-trimmed coat, a garment worn by scholars and gentlemen. He further affirms his learning by writing the inscription in Latin, not German. It reads, "I, Albrecht Dürer of Nuremberg, painted myself thus, with undying colors, at the age of twenty-eight years." The pose was taken from images of Christ, but most art historians do not see this as sacrilegious or blasphemous. Instead, they view it as Dürer's clearest statement about the creative power of the artist, a power through which artists can become God-like, but that ultimately comes from God. Along with many portraits, Dürer produced woodcuts, engravings, and etchings that rendered the human form and the natural world in amazing detail, and wrote treatises on proportion and measurement.

Raphael, *Portrait of Pope Leo X with Two Cardinals, circa 1518–1519*

In this portrait, Pope Leo X (born Giovanni de Medici, one of the sons of Lorenzo shown as a little boy in Ghirlandaio's fresco in the Sassetti Chapel) is flanked by two of his nephews who were cardinals. Raphael portrays the pope dressed in rich velvet with an illuminated book and carved bell in front of him, indications of Leo's patronage of the arts. Shortly before he painted this, Raphael had received the commission for frescoes in the papal apartments and been put in charge of the building of St. Peter's Basilica. Although Leo was his patron and friend, Raphael does not idealize him here, but shows him with a chunky body and puffy face. The somewhat anxious expressions on the faces might reflect church officials' growing awareness of troubles in the church coming from Germany, where Martin Luther was beginning to criticize the methods of papal tax collection that were providing funds for the building of St. Peter's. In his relatively short life, Raphael painted hundreds of portraits and devotional images, becoming the most sought-after artist in Europe. He also oversaw a large workshop with many collaborators and apprentices—who assisted on the less difficult sections of some paintings—and wrote treatises on his philosophy of art, in which he emphasized the importance of imitating nature and developing an orderly sequence of design and proportion, which he called *buona maniera* (good style).

Fra Fillipo Lippi, *Portrait of a Man and Woman at a Casement, 1440s*

This double portrait of a wealthy man and woman in Florence was probably painted to commemorate their wedding or the birth of their first child. Wedding portraits, either with the couple painted together as they are here or in two separate frames, became increasingly popular in the later fifteenth century. Jewels such as those the woman wears were often handed down from generation to generation within families, just as the family land viewed through the window was handed down. The placement of the figures is enigmatic, but might have represented men's responsibility for family business outside of the house and women's more domestic concerns. The woman's figure suggests she is pregnant, which might have been the case if this commemorates a birth, but a rounded stomach was also the style in the mid-fifteenth century, so this could simply be her clothing.

Andrea Mantegna, *Family of Ludovico II Gonzaga*, 1465–1474

Andrea Mantegna was the court painter for the Gonzaga family who ruled the city-state of Mantua in northern Italy. In this fresco, painted in a room in the ducal palace of Mantua, he shows Duke Ludovico with his wife Barbara of Brandenburg (the daughter of the Holy Roman Emperor), some of their children, and a number of courtiers and officials. He even includes the court dwarf—the very small woman to the right of the seated Barbara—a common figure in Renaissance courts because people were interested in what they saw as human oddities. Mantegna places the figures in a setting that looks like a stage, allowing him to demonstrate his skill with perspective and foreshortening, the portrayal of three-dimensional figures on a two-dimensional surface in proportions that match those seen by the eye. Ludovico is in informal dress, and the family itself is arranged in fairly intimate poses, but the rigid stance of many of the courtiers, and the fact that the duke is doing business even while in the midst of his family, reminded those who saw the painting that families such as the Gonzagas were the basis of the state and never really private.

Bronzino, *Eleanor of Toledo and Her Son*, 1544–1545

Agnolo Bronzino became the official court painter to Duke Cosimo I Medici in about 1540, and painted a number of portraits of the duke and members of his court. His portrait of Cosimo's wife Eleanor of Toledo—a Spanish noblewoman whose father was ruler of the Kingdom of Naples in southern Italy—shows her with her oldest son, the heir to the Medici duchy. Her husband might have ordered the portrait to symbolize stability and continuity in the Medici line, but Eleanor herself probably ordered the dress, which was her wedding dress and might have been the dress in which she was buried. The elaborate brocade of the dress almost overpowers the duchess, but Bronzino does capture some of what we know from other sources was her calm strength. She eventually had eleven children—eight of whom survived—and her husband often named her regent, or acting ruler, when he was away from Florence.

Lavinia Fontana, *Portrait of a Family*, circa 1585

Lavinia Fontana, the daughter of a painter, received commissions to paint single portraits and family groups in her native Bologna and other Italian cities. Here the men's lace collars and the women's red coral beads indicate their wealth, and the dog—a symbol of loyalty—and the protective gestures suggest family bonds. As was common in family portraits, even in those arranged somewhat informally as was this one, the males are on one side and the females on the other. Fontana is one of a handful of female painters from the Renaissance whose names are known. Most female painters were, like her, the daughters of painters, trained by their fathers. Women were not allowed to study the male nude, which was viewed as essential if one wanted to paint large history paintings with many figures, so they generally painted portraits, smaller paintings with only a few subjects, or still lifes and interior scenes. Women could also not learn the technique of fresco, in which colors are applied directly to wet plaster walls, because such works had to be done out in public, which was judged inappropriate for women.

Lucas van Leyden, *Family of Beggars on the Road*, 1520

Most illustrations of families in the Renaissance show the rich and powerful, for artists generally worked on commission and only wealthy families could afford to have their portraits painted. Some artists also depicted more ordinary families and even the poor, however, providing social commentary through their art. Here Lucas van Leyden, a Dutch artist renowned especially for his engravings and etchings, shows a family of beggars on the road. Steep inflation in the sixteenth century led to an increase in the number of families who could not pay their rent, and who therefore took to the roads looking for work or charity. City officials worried about what they termed "sturdy beggars," vagabonds with no fixed place of residence who they thought likely to engage in crime. Leyden portrays this family somewhat sympathetically, for they are certainly not shown as threatening. He does not show them as particularly downtrodden, however, and perhaps suggests through the large number of children and the father's playing the bagpipe that their circumstances are to some degree their own fault.

CHAPTER 5

Merchants and Master Craftsmen

Customers and shopkeepers bargain in a narrow Italian city street specifically set up for fabric and furniture merchants. In the foreground of this fifteenth-century book illustration are stalls selling cloth and clothing, and in the background are stalls with wooden benches and chests.

Renaissance artists portrayed individuals and their environment in great detail, and nothing received as much care in their works as material objects. Renaissance paintings are bursting with ornately carved chairs, deep-plushed tapestries, inlaid cabinets, and marble statuettes. Portraits show their subjects wearing colorful silk stockings, golden belts, pearl earrings, velvet jackets, brocade cloaks, and elaborate hats. And that's the men! Such luxury represented an ideal, of course, in the same way that many portraits show idealized facial features, with little sign of worries or aging. But luxurious material goods were also a reality for many people, brought in from China or Southeast Asia though the trading networks of the Indian Ocean, or made closer to home in the workshops of goldsmiths, tailors, silk weavers, and furniture makers.

Where did the money to buy luxuries come from? Primarily from the profit gained through buying and selling things and through handling money. In this, the Renaissance economy was much like our own postindustrial economy, with vast fortunes made in international business and banking.

The expansion of trade began before the Renaissance, in the eleventh century when merchants began to import luxuries such as spices and silks. They started to keep increasingly elaborate records of their transactions, and devised new methods of bookkeeping to keep track of their ventures. As trade grew, merchants devised ways to pool their resources and talents, formalizing these agreements with various forms of contracts, including permanent arrangements called in Italian compagnie. (Compagnie literally means "bread together," that is, sharing bread, and is the root of the English word "company.") They joined together in merchants' guilds, and as cities grew, served in city governments so that urban economic policies served merchant interests. Trading companies sponsored land and sea expeditions, and hired ship-builders to design and construct ships that were bigger, faster, and more seaworthy. Italian merchants developed permanent trading centers in most of the ports of the Middle East and north Africa. Through these business activities, merchants created the economic system based on private ownership, competition, and profit that was later called capital-ism, and today is found in most of the world. Historians often call this expansion and transformation of the European economy the Commer-cial Revolution, because of its long-term effects on society.

The expansion of business in the Renaissance created great op-portunities, but it also created a moral problem. In the early Middle Ages, the Christian church in the West had forbidden usury, the charg-ing of interest on a loan. In the agricultural economy of the period, loans were intended mainly for consumption—tiding someone over until the next harvest, for example. Theologians reasoned it was wrong for Chris-tians to take advantage of the bad luck or need of other Christians, so loans should be made pro amore (out of love), not with an eye to profit. Christian authorities often prohibited Jews from owning land or engag-ing in most kinds of business, so in some parts of Europe Jews became money-lenders, which increased resentment against them.

As commerce grew, loans were increasingly for investment rather than consumption, and the bankers and merchants who made them did so to earn a profit, not out of concern for their fellow man. Because of the prohibition of usury, however, they often hid the interest in con-tracts. Gradually the Church relaxed its sanction against charging interest, declaring that some interest was legitimate as a payment for the risk the investor was taking and only interest above a certain level would be considered usury. (Today's usury laws, usually issued by state governments, also define an upper allowable limit for interest rates.) The stigma attached to money-lending did not disappear completely, however, and merchants were advised to give to the Church, limit their profits to what would be considered fair, and not flaunt their wealth.

Some newly wealthy people did avoid conspicuous consumption, but portraits show that most did not. Cities also tried firmer measures, passing regulations called sumptuary laws, which were essentially urban dress codes requiring or prohibiting people to dress in certain ways. Only nobles and wealthy urban residents could wear fine silk clothing, jewelry, and bright colors, whereas artisans were to wear linen garments, and servants were restricted to rough dark clothes and aprons. Fines were set for breaking these laws, but they were never easy to enforce. Govern-

ments also encouraged people to wear locally made cloth and clothing instead of imported luxuries through taxes on imports, which proved to be more effective than sumptuary laws in shaping clothing choices.

When trade expanded in the Commercial Revolution, Eastern luxuries such as spices and silks were paid for primarily in gold, but this created an unfavorable balance of trade. Italian merchants sought a product for which there would be high demand, and discovered it in quality woolen cloth. They organized its production in the same way they organized their trading ventures, as a capitalist enterprise, purchasing raw materials, hiring workers for all stages of production, and then selling the finished cloth. Most stages of production were carried out in people's homes, not in large factories, but the merchants owned the materials at every stage, and set prices and wages.

In the thirteenth and fourteenth centuries, cloth workers challenged the merchants' control through strikes and revolts, and attempted to form their own organizations, called craft guilds. The cloth merchants in some areas, such as Florence, were successful at stopping all organizing and suppressing all rebellions, but in other places the merchants lost, and the wool workers were able to form their own guilds. At the same time, those who produced many other sorts of products, such as shoemakers, goldsmiths, and armor makers, recognized the benefits of organization, and also formed separate craft guilds. In craft guilds, the master craftsman who carried out the actual work owned the raw materials, the tools, and the finished product. Thus side-by-side with merchant capitalism, a very different organization of production, craft guilds, developed in late medieval and Renaissance Europe.

The economic expansion and attention to the material world of the Renaissance did not mean that people turned away from religious devotion. Merchants' and craft guilds maintained altars at city churches and provided for religious rituals such as baptisms, funerals, and celebrations of the guild's patron saint. They provided charity for the poor, and took problems in the church very seriously.

The Commercial Revolution

Contracts between wealthy merchants involved large sums, but sometimes quite ordinary people invested small amounts in trading ventures. In this contract drawn up in the Italian city of Genoa in 1198, some of the investors are of such low social standing that they do not have last names, but are simply known by their occupation. The two men who actually went on the voyage from Genoa to Corsica and Sardinia—not a very far distance—put up tiny amounts of money, but gained a greater share of the profits because of the time and effort they put in.

The inhabitants of this city are for the most part engaged in commerce, and indeed they are great merchants and are very rich. . . . They are capable of dwelling and carrying on business throughout the world. Most of them, and even the women (though they may not have been out of the country) know how to speak three or four languages, not to mention those who speak five and six and seven; this is something to marvel at as well as a great advantage.

—The Italian humanist and historian Ludovico Guicciardini, describing the northern European city of Antwerp in a survey of cities for Italian travelers, 1560

Genoa, December 22, 1198

We, Embone of Sozziglia and Master Alberto, acknowledge that we carry for the purpose of trading £ 142 Genoese to the port of Bonifacio and through or in Corsica and Sardinia; and from there we are to come [back]. And of this [sum], £ 25 Genoese belong to you, Giordano Clerico; and £ 10 to you, Oberto Croce. And to you, Vasallo Rapallino, [belong] £ 10; and to you, Bonsignore Torre, £ 10. And £ 5 [belong] to Pietro Bonfante; and to you, Michele, tanner, [belong] £ 5; and to you Giovanni del Pero, £ 5; and to Ara Dolce, £ 6; and to Ansaldo Mirto, £ 5; and to Martino, hemp-seller, £ 5; and to Ansaldo Fanti, £ 8; and to you, Lanfranco of Crosa, £ 20; and to Josbert, nephew of Charles of Bensançon, £ 10. And £ 6 belong to me, Embrone; and £ 2 to me, Alberto. And all the pounds mentioned above are to be profitably employed and invested, and they are to draw by the pound [that is, each investor receives profits proportional to the investment]. And we promise to send [back] the capital and the profit which God shall have granted from this [contract].

International trade brought the possibility of profit, but it also carried a variety of risks. The diary of Gregorio Dati, an important Florentine merchant who died in 1435, describes many of these, ranging from the exotic to the mundane. Dati regularly travelled on business for a company in which he was a partner, and his trips sometimes ended in disaster.

I set out for Valencia in September 1393 in order to wind up matters there but did not get beyond Genoa. When I reached the Riviera, I was set upon and robbed by a galley from Briganzone and returned to Florence on 14 December, having lost 250 florins' worth of pearls, merchandise and clothes belonging to myself, and 300 gold florins' worth of the company's property.

Gregorio Dati's brother Simone, also a partner in the firm, had even worse luck on his own trip to Valencia, when his ship met a warship of King Louis of France, who was trying to assert his claim to the throne of Naples in southern Italy and needed cash.

Ships crowd into the port of Lisbon in the sixteenth century in an engraving by the artist Theodore de Bry, who later became famous for his depictions of indigenous people in the New World. Here de Bry captures the bustle of activity common in any seaport, with chests, casks, and bundles of goods being loaded and unloaded.

Simone left here for Valencia on 3 January and, having set sail from Pisa on the 8th, was captured by one of King Louis's admirals, Messer Giovanni Gonsalvo of Seville, who took him as a prisoner to Naples. When he had been held there for three months, he was taken to Gaeta and released for a ransom of 200 florins. This was paid for him by Doffo Spini, whom we reimbursed, and debited to the Valencian account with a number of other expenses.

As the voyages of the Dati brothers indicate, merchants in the Mediterranean were prey to bandits and local conflicts. Those planning longer voyages recognized that the threats could be even greater, and took steps to protect their vessels. About a decade after Simone Dati's capture, Genoese officials in charge of shipping issued the following proclamation regarding a ship bound for Chios, an island in the Aegean Sea off the coast of Turkey.

Genoa, September 1, 1408
We, Officers of the Sea or of the Provisions for the Genoese Shipping, make it known and attest to each and all persons who shall see the present letter that in order to protect the ship of the nobleman Megollo Lercari, which is preparing to sail to the Orient, in such a way as to render futile the assaults of any corsairs [pirates], we have now increased through the said patron Megollo the usual crew of said ship, which consists of 73 men, by 25 arbalesters [soldiers armed with cross-bows] for the present voyage as far as Chios. And the scribe of the said ship is to be required to keep a separate account in regard to them. And the expenses of these 25 arbalesters—the usual food and living costs and salary and the other expenses which shall be specified—are to be paid from said ship and [precisely] from the freight charge and from merchandise now loaded or going to be loaded in the said ship for the present voyage destined for Gaeta, Naples, and other ports beyond Naples in the direction of parts east and south.

Pirates and the possibility of capture were serious problems, but most issues facing Renaissance business agreements were more mundane. As merchant Gregorio Dati records in his diary, these included disagreements between partners and bad business decisions.

I have agreed with Michele to send his son Giovanni to Valencia, where he is to form a business partnership with Simone for as long as we shall decide. We will supply the goods they require and our firm will put 1,000 florins cash at their disposal. One half of whatever profits they make will be ours, and the other half is to be divided

Jacob Fugger the Rich
Italian merchants were the first to use the new business methods, but merchants in other parts of Europe were quick to learn and prosper. One of the most successful was Jacob Fugger, a merchant-banker from Augsburg in southern Germany. He began by selling cloth, but realized that the greatest opportunity for profit came from money-lending. Jacob Fugger loaned money to nobles, church leaders, and rulers, accepting control of mines as security on the loans. He gradually established a monopoly of silver and copper mining in central Europe. The profit from the mines was recirculated into further loans, and Fugger made an enormous fortune; his contemporaries called him "Jacob the Rich." He financed the imperial election of Charles V—a Hapsburg—in 1519, and four years later felt bold enough to write directly to the emperor, asking for the repayment of the loan, commenting, "It is well known and clear as day that your Imperial Majesty could not have acquired the Roman Crown without my help." His letter even included a veiled threat: "If I had remained aloof from the house of Austria [the Hapsburgs] and had served France, I would have obtained much profit and money, which was then offered to me. Your majesty may well ponder with deep understanding the damage which would have resulted for your Imperial Majesty and the house of Austria." Charles could not repay him, but instead gave him control of mercury and silver mines in Spain and the Americas.

A bird's-eye view of the city of Amsterdam in the sixteenth century shows ships crowded in the protected harbor and many others moored just offshore, sending merchandise to shore in small boats. Shipping goods by water was much cheaper than shipping by land, and merchants were willing to risk the possibility of pirate attacks or shipwreck because of the opportunities for profits.

between them, so that each will have one quarter of the total profits. Giovanni went to Valencia in May 1396, but only stayed there a short time as he did not get on with Simone . . . . Giovanni and Simone continued to wrangle and bicker even more than before, until finally Giovanni resolved to leave for Barcelona and to settle there. . . .

At this point, fortune turned against me. Simone had gone into business on his own account in Valencia and was involved in transactions with the King of Castile. I let him have great quantities of merchandise and bills of exchange for large sums of money. I had been against his engaging in this activity, but he was convinced that he was right. He let our company in for trouble, litigation, and losses so that we went deeply into debt and were on the point of going bankrupt....

[A]lthough my partner was in favour of going bankrupt so as to avoid some losses and expenditure, I was resolved to face ruin rather than loss of honor. I held out so firmly and struggled to such purpose that in the end we managed to pay all our debts, and I satisfied all claims except those of my partners. May God be praised and blessed.

Families and Fortunes

As Dati's diary indicates, many business connections were also family connections—brothers partnered with brothers, fathers set their sons up in business, and cousins, uncles, and nephews assisted one another. Female family members did not go on trading ventures, for their freedom to travel was generally limited by family responsibilities and by the lack of places for female travelers to stay. Female family members were not completely excluded, however. Sometimes, especially when they were widows, they invested money that they had inherited or acquired through marriage, or bought and sold property on their own. The wealthy Florentine widow Alessandra Strozzi, for example, wrote to her twenty-year-old son Lorenzo in 1453 that she was thinking about selling one of her properties to help him and his brother Filippo start a business, although she had heard things about his behavior that made her wonder if this was a wise idea.

I'd been thinking of selling the farm at Antella to get rid of a lot of expense and aggravation and to help you [all] get on. Once what's owing on it has been paid it would bring in a clear eight hundred florins. Filippo has another three hundred and I'd thought of you and Filippo using the money for business ventures so you could start to accumulate some capital. [But] from all I hear you know more about throwing money away

In this portrait of an Italian merchant and his family, the Italian artist Lorenzo Lotto suggests the source of the family's wealth with the Turkish carpet on the table and the sea in the background. The wife and daughter wear elegant satin dresses that are similar in style, and the infant son reaches for cherries in his father's hand in a gesture that also suggests that the family business will one day pass from his father's hands to his.

than about saving a penny, and it should be the opposite. I can see you've done us harm and brought us shame, and yourself too. I gather you've got some bad habits and lecturing you does no good at all.

Dati's diary provides examples of another way that women were integrated into the flow of capital: their dowries. Women of all classes were expected to bring a dowry to their marriage, which might consist of some clothing and household items (usually including the marriage bed and bedding) for poor women, or vast amounts of cash, goods, or property for wealthy ones. Dati married four times, and each time his wife brought him a sizable dowry. His first wife died after a miscarriage, and three years later he married his second wife, as he notes in his diary.

I shall record here how I married my second wife, Isabetta, known as Betta . . . . On 31 March 1393, I was betrothed to her and on Easter Monday, 7 April, I gave her the ring. On 22 June, a Sunday, I became her husband in the name of God and good fortune. Her first cousins, Giovanni and Lionardo di Domenico Arrighi, promised that she should have a dowry of 900 gold florins and that, apart from the dowry, she should have the income on a farm in S. Fiore a Elsa, which had been left her as a legacy by her mother, Monna Veronica.

This seven-foot-long wedding chest made of cedar and painted with gold leaf contained some of the goods that a wealthy Italian woman brought to her husband as part of her dowry on marriage in the late fifteenth century. At the time of the wedding, these chests were transported from the father's house to the husband's, where they also served as pieces of furniture.

Betta gave birth to eight children, four of whom died in infancy, and she died herself after nine years of marriage. Dati expressed grief at his wife's death, but this could not last long. Marriage was an economic as well as an emotional matter in Renaissance Italy, and four months after Isabetta's death, Dati was hoping a new dowry could bring the money needed to begin a new business. Dati was successful in the search for a third wife he describes here, who brought him money and more children, as did his fourth wife.

I have undertaken to put up 2,000 florins. This is how I propose to raise them: 1,370 florins and 25 soldi a fiorino are still due to me

The painted side panel of a magnificent wedding chest brought by a Florentine bride as part of her dowry shows a wedding procession, with couples walking under a banner. The last couple, with the man holding out his hand and the woman wearing a wreath on her head, is the bride and groom, and might represent Petrarch and Laura, the woman who inspired his love poetry when he saw her across a room. He probably never spoke to her, and she died young, so images of the two as a couple became symbols of love conquering all, even death.

This sixteenth-century miniature shows a beautifully dressed woman weaving a complicated pattern. It is not a portrayal of the actual conditions for weavers at the time, which were often harsh, but a portrait of the ancient Greek heroine Penelope, the wife of Ulysses. When her husband did not return from the Trojan War, Penelope promised to marry one of her suitors when she finished her weaving, but she unraveled her work every night so this never happened, and Ulysses finally returned. Penelope was often used as an example of the faithful wife in the Renaissance, and weaving itself symbolized virtue and chastity.

from my old partnership with Michele di Ser Parente, as appears on page 118 of my ledger for stock and cash on hand. The rest I expect to obtain if I marry again this year, when I hope to find a woman with a dowry as large as God may be pleased to grant me. If I do not marry, I will find some money some other way.

Merchants and Morality

Although disaster was always a possibility, the opportunities for financial gain in business were much larger in the Renaissance than they had been earlier, but many people remained uncomfortable with the idea that the investment of money, rather than skill or effort, should bring a profit. Merchants and bankers were advised to consider morality as well as money in their business dealings. In *The Practice of Commerce*, the fourteenth-century Florentine merchant Francesco di Balduccio Pegolotti includes a poem setting out the qualities that an ideal virtuous merchant should both possess and demonstrate to others.

> A merchant wishing that his worth be great
> Must always act according as is right;
> And let him be a man of long foresight,
> And never fail his promises to keep.
>   Let him be pleasant, if he can, of looks,
> As fits the honor'd calling that he chose;
> Open when selling, but when buying close;
> Genial in greeting and without complaints.
>   He will be worthier if he goes to church,
> Gives for the love of God, clinches his deals
> Without a haggle, and wholly repeals
> Usury taking. Further he must write
> Accounts well-kept and free from oversight.

Dati's diary provides us with a glimpse of how one merchant felt he measured up to the ideal of a moral and pious merchant as set out by Pegolotti and others. Most of Dati's comments about the spiritual side of life are formulaic: "In the name of God, his Mother and all the Saints of Paradise" the diary opens, a phrase that is regularly repeated. In this he follows a pattern set by earlier Italian merchants, such as the renowned Francesco Datini, who headed every account book and ledger with "in the name of God and profit." On New Years' Day 1404, however, Dati sets out a series of resolutions for himself. The final sentence indicates that Dati does not intend this to be a legally binding contract like those he made to set up a company, and in setting fines for himself if he breaks his resolutions he anticipates his inability to stick to them. We might view this as a typical

Hans Holbein's double portrait, painted in 1533, shows the French ambassador to the English court, dressed in a satin shirt and fur-lined coat, along with a French bishop who was on a diplomatic mission in London. The men are surrounded by objects representing the arts, sciences, trade, and exploration, and this appears to be a celebration of the glories of wealth and power. The strange object at the ambassador's feet, however, is a skewed skull that morphs into shape when seen from far to one side of the painting. This might have been Holbein's comment on the fleetingness of human life, but it might also have been simply Holbein showing off his skill as a painter who could handle complex issues of perspective, for he never explained it.

midlife crisis—a forty-year-old businessman worrying about life's greater meaning, but not quite willing to give up on what could lead to success. Nevertheless, they portray a man thinking a bit more about God and less about profit.

I know that in this wretched life our sins expose us to many tribulations of soul and of passions of the body, that without God's grace and mercy which strengthens our weakness, enlightens our mind and supports our will, we would perish daily. I also see that since my birth forty years ago, I have given little heed to God's commandments. Distrusting my own power to reform, but hoping to advance by degrees along the path of virtue, I resolve from this day forward to refrain from going to the shop or conducting business on solemn Church holidays, or from permitting others to work for me or seek temporal gain on such days. Whenever I make exceptions in cases of extreme necessity, I promise, on the following day, to distribute alms of one gold florin to God's poor. I have written this down so that I may remember my promise and be ashamed if I should chance to break it.

Also, in memory of the passion of Our Lord Jesus Christ who freed and saved us by His merits, that He may, by His grace and mercy preserve us from guilty passions, I resolve from this very day and in perpetuity to keep Friday as a day of total chastity—with Friday I include the following night—when I must abstain from the enjoyment of all carnal pleasures. God give me the grace to keep my promise, yet if I should break it through forgetfulness, I engage to give 20 soldi to the poor for each time, and to say twenty Our Fathers and Ave Marias.

I resolve this day to do a third thing while I am in health and able to, remembering that each day we need Almighty God to provide for us. Each day I wish to honor God by some giving of alms or by the recitation of prayers or some other pious act. If, by inadvertence, I fail to do so, that day or the next day I must give alms to God's poor of at least 5 soldi. These however are not vows but intentions by which I shall do my best to abide.

Jews in Renaissance Cities

The expansion of commerce created an arena for Christian–Jewish conflict in the Renaissance. In early medieval society, Jews in many areas had performed important economic functions, loaning money and acting as bankers for their Christian neighbors, including rulers. In return they received the right to live and do business in certain places, although this could be revoked at any time when a ruler changed his or her mind. Jews were expelled from England in the thirteenth century and briefly from France in the fourteenth. In 1492, King Ferdinand and Queen Isabella ordered all Jews to leave Spain or convert. After the expulsions, many Jews migrated to Italy, where some city rulers invited Jews in to help expand foreign trade. Christian merchants often objected to this, as a 1412 report to the rulers of Venice about complaints at the nearby city of Retimo suggests.

Some noble citizens and vassals of our locality of Retimo are making complaints. They have explained that the Jews of said locality, not content with the interest and the incalculable profit that they obtain from usuries and contracts, capture all profit and proceeds that are obtained from the art and profession of commerce in that locality, so much so that one could say that these very Jews are lords of the money and of the men of that locality and district; and further, that these very Jews occupy nearly all the stalls, shops,

A Jewish family holds a seder, the festive meal that marks the beginning of Passover, in a fifteenth-century manuscript from Frankfurt in Germany. Even though this manuscript was written in Hebrew, and so designed for a Jewish readership, the artist was careful to show the father wearing the hat prescribed by the Christian officials of the city.

and stores, both those located on the square of Retimo and those around and near that square; and this brings very great harm upon our faithful and their utter destitution, because only these very Jews sell and dispose of their merchandise, and our citizens, being unable to have the said shops, are not able to sell anything or have any proceeds.

Christian complaints about Jewish merchants were exaggerated, but to calm Christian fears Italian rulers began to segregate Jews in walled ghettoes. They also obliged Jews to wear specific symbols on their clothes or hats of a specific color, so that they would be easily recognizable. These regulations of Jewish clothing were part of the broader sumptuary laws, through which authorities tried to restrict the clothing worn by all sorts of groups. In 1595, an official in a small town ruled by the city of Genoa complained in a letter to the Genoese city council that Angelo Nantua, a Jewish money-lender, was not taking the law very seriously. In turning what was a mark of separation into a fashionable piece of clothing, Angelo Nantua was following a common Renaissance pattern. For example, along with Jews, prostitutes were often ordered to wear something yellow—the color of the flames of hell—so that their "dishonorable" status could be seen by all, but they then used yellow satin and feathers to trim flattering capes and hats, attracting the eyes of potential customers.

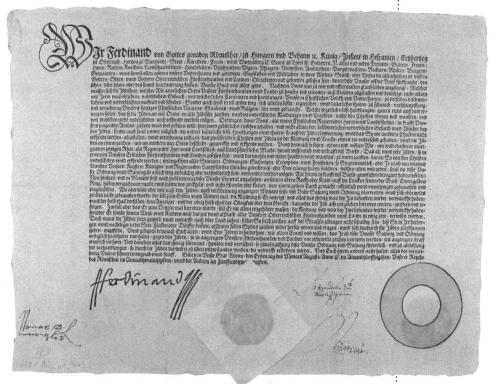

With this decree from 1551, the Holy Roman Emperor Ferdinand I ordered all Jews, male and female, to wear a yellow ring of cloth on their outer garments whenever they were in the towns he controlled. The ring was to be no smaller than the size shown on the original document, about 5 inches across. If they did not, their clothing and all that they had with them was to be confiscated, with half going to the person who reported them and half to the authorities. The third time they were discovered without the ring, they were to be banished from the entire empire forever.

Most Serene and Excellent Sirs and Honorable Patrons,

By the orders of your most serene Excellencies it remains obligatory that the Jews who reside in this land must permanently wear a hat or cap of yellow color under penalty of a twenty lire fine for each transgression. . . . But the said Angelo wore a hat made of taffeta of golden color, decorated with a black veil outside and lined with black taffeta on the inside, of such beauty that it was closer to a ceremonious style than to anything else. I don't know if it is of the mind of your most serene Excellencies that he should therefore be punished or how, but I also wish to inform you that the Jews in Pallodio [another nearby town] have been wearing the black hat [of Christians] without being punished, it seems for ten years, much to the scandal of the people of the town.

Clothing and Capitalism

Sumptuary laws set out a hierarchy of wealth and marked certain groups as outsiders, and they also attempted to limit frivolous spending on luxuries and promote local production. English sumptuary laws issued by Queen Elizabeth I in 1574 laid out all the dangers posed by the increase in foreign trade.

The excess of apparel and the superfluity of unnecessary foreign wares thereto belonging now of late years is grown to such an extremity that the manifest decay of the whole realm generally is like to

In this engraving by a Dutch artist from the late sixteenth century, English women of different social classes wear the dress appropriate to their status, from middle-class market women to wealthy aristocrats. The engraving is an idealization, not a depiction of reality, for authorities had great difficulty enforcing sumptuary laws that prohibited people from dressing "above their station," especially when increased foreign trade made luxuries like silk ribbons, feathers, and lace so cheap that even domestic servants could afford them.

Virgo Anglica.   *Mercatorum uxores.*   *Nobiles mulieres Anglicæ.*   *Nobilis aulica.*

follow (by bringing into the realm such superfluities of silks, cloths of gold, silver, and other most vain devices of so great cost that the moneys and treasure of the realm is and must be yearly conveyed out of the same to pay for the said excess) but also particularly the wasting and undoing of a great number of young gentlemen, otherwise serviceable, and others seeking by show of apparel to be esteemed as gentlemen, who, allured by the vain show of those things, do not only consume themselves, their goods, and lands which their parents left unto them, but also run into such debts and shifts as they cannot live out of danger of laws without attempting unlawful acts, whereby they are not any ways serviceable to their country as otherwise they might be.

Craft Guilds

Beginning in the thirteenth century, craft guilds took over the regulation of production from the merchant guilds or developed their own systems. They set quality standards for their particular product; regulated the size of workshops, the training period, and the conduct of members; and set up systems of overseers and officers. The spurriers' (spurmakers') guild of London addressed other issues as well in its 1345 ordinances, including the dangers of working at night.

In the first place, no one of the trade of spurriers shall work longer than from the beginning of the day until curfew rings out at the church of St. Sepulcher, without [outside of the city gate called] Newgate; by reason that no man can work so neatly by night as by day. And many persons of the said trade, who compass [know] how to practice deception in their work, desire to work by night rather than by day; and then they introduce false iron, and iron that has been cracked, for tin, and also they put gilt on false copper, and cracked.

And further, many of the said trade are wandering about all day, without working at all at their trade; and then, when they have become drunk and frantic, they take to their work, to the annoyance of the sick and all their neighborhood as well, by reason of the broils [fights] that arise between them and the strange folk who are dwelling among them. And then they blow up their fires so vigorously, that their forges begin all at once to blaze, to the great peril of themselves and of all the neighborhood around. And then, too, all the neighbors are much in dread of the sparks, which so vigorously issue forth in all directions from the mouths of the chimneys in their forges.

His wares on display above him, a saddler shapes the wooden support for a saddle while a customer looks on. The rhyme beneath the woodcut notes that he makes saddles for all types of people, including knights in jousting tournaments and fine ladies, but also farmers and carters. This woodcut appeared in a series of illustrations of the craft guilds in southern Germany in the early sixteenth century, and shows the conditions of a workshop quite accurately.

By reason thereof it seems unto them that working by night should be put an end to, in order to avoid such false work and such perils; and therefore the mayor and the aldermen do will, by the assent of the good folk of the said trade and for the common profit, that from henceforth such time for working, and such false work made in the trade, shall be forbidden. And if any person shall be found in the said trade to do the contrary hereof, let him be amerced [fined], the first time in forty pence . . . and the fourth time, let him forswear the trade forever.

Also, that no one of the said trade shall take an apprentice for a less term than seven years.

Each guild set the pattern by which members were trained. For the London spurriers, one began with seven years as an apprentice; other guilds set out different periods, and by the late sixteenth century apprenticeships were often formalized by a contract written up by a notary. Once a young man had finished his apprenticeship, he then worked as a journeyman in the shops of other masters for a set period of years, after which he could theoretically make his masterpiece. If the masterpiece was approved by the other master craftsmen and if they thought the market was large enough in their town to allow for another master in the craft, he could then become a master and start a shop. In this contract from 1610 in Paris, a woman whose husband had deserted her apprentices her son with a master ribbon and trim maker.

Marie Frevel, wife but deserted for the last nine years, she says, by Mahis Deslandres, master ribbon and trim maker in Paris . . . affirms that, for the benefit of Adam Deslandres, son of the said Mahis Deslandres and of the said Frevel, aged 11 years or so, whom the said Frevel has pledged to complete faithfulness and loyalty, she has given and placed him in service and employment for the next three years. [She has placed him] with the respectable Henry Camue, master of the said trade of ribbon and trim maker in Paris.

Camue has taken and retained Adam Deslandres in his service for the said time, during which he will be obliged and promises to show and teach him Camue's trade and all in which he is involved because of it; supply and deliver what he needs in terms of fire, bed, lodging, and light, and treat him gently, as is appropriate.

And Frevel will maintain him during the said time with all clothing, linen, footwear, and other respectable clothing, according to his status.

In consideration of this service, the said parties remain in agreement on the sum of 18 livres tournois that the said Camue promises and guarantees to pay to the said Frevel . . .

·CHRISTO · SACRVM ·
ILLe·Dei verbo·magna pietate·favebat·
·perpetva·dignvs·posteritate·coli·

·D·FRIDR·DVCI·SAXON·S·R·IMP·
·ARCHIM·ELECTORI·
·Albertvs·dvrer·Nvr·faciebat·
·B·M·F·V·V·
·M·D·XXIIII·

In this 1524 engraving by Albrecht Dürer, Duke Frederick the Wise of Saxony wears items of clothing that would each have been made by a separate guild. His felt hat was made by members of the hat-makers guild, his fur-trimmed coat by the furriers, and his linen shirt by the tailors.

To make this agreement, present was the said employee, who has promised to serve his said master faithfully, work to his benefit, and warn him of losses as soon as they should come to the boy's attention; and not to run away nor go to serve elsewhere during the said time.

And in case of flight or absence, the said Frevel promises to search in the city and outskirts of Paris and bring her son back if she can find him, to complete the time of his said service.

The master's wife assisted in running the shop, often selling the goods her husband had produced, and their children worked alongside the apprentices and journeymen. Girls were sometimes apprenticed on their

An illustration from an early printed book about how to raise children shows an urban family working together. The mother—who is rocking an infant's cradle with her foot—teaches her daughter to spin, while the father teaches a young son to do math, using a book and a counting tool.

own, especially in crafts such as silk-making or hat-making, but in general girls and women fit into the guild system more often through their relations with male guild members than on their own. Most guilds allowed a master's widow to continue operating a shop for a set period of time after her husband's death, for they recognized she had the necessary skills and experience. Widows paid all guild dues, but they did not vote or hold office in the guilds because they were not considered full members. The brief section about widows in the 1535 ordinances of the goldsmiths of the German city of Nuremberg, added almost as an afterthought, is typical of guild considerations of what was a very common situation.

If, when a goldsmith dies, there is no son who wants to inherit the shop or continue on in the craft, or none who is skilled or old enough to make the masterpiece at that time, his widow will be allowed to continue the shop (if she wants) three years after the death of her husband and no longer, unless she marries someone who is a master goldsmith or who makes his masterpiece during this time. Every widow who is continuing a shop will have to obey all the guild ordinances and bring her work to be inspected, and be liable to the same fines as a master if she breaks any regulations.

Both craft and merchants' guilds were not only economic organizations, but also systems of social support. The 1346 ordinances of the London white-tawyers' guild, who processed leather with salt, alum, and other substances so that it had a white surface, set out a system of support for elderly masters and widows. In these provisions, the white-tawyers combined economic aims and religious observance, in the same way that merchants combined "God and profit" in their account books.

In the first place, the white tawyers have ordained that they will find a wax candle, to burn before our Lady in the church of Allhallows, near London wall.

Also, that each person of the said trade shall put in the box such sum as he shall think fit, in aid of maintaining the said candle.

Also, if by chance any one of the said trade shall fall into poverty, whether through old age or because he cannot labor or work, and have nothing with which to keep himself, he shall have every week from the said box 7d. for his support, if he be a man of good repute. And after his decease, if he have a wife, a woman of good repute, she shall have weekly for her support 7d. from the said box, so long as she shall behave herself well and keep single.

CHAPTER 6

Religious Reform and Renewal

During the fifteenth century, writers, artists, and musicians celebrated the glory of the world, and merchants found ready buyers for their luxurious clothing and household goods. This did not mean, however, that people paid attention only to the material world around them. As they had for centuries, they also thought about the world to come and about their obligations to God, and their days often included activities with religious meaning and purposes. The vast majority of people in Europe were Christian, and the calendar was set according to Christian periods and days, with the lives of Christ, the Virgin Mary, and various saints marked in an annual cycle of special holy days (or holidays).

The Church taught that certain rituals, called sacraments, brought God's grace, the divine assistance needed to lead a good Christian life and to merit salvation. Seven sacraments—baptism, penance, the Eucharist, confirmation, marriage, priestly ordination, and anointment of the dying—had been formally accepted by a church council in the thirteenth century, so that most of life's transitions were marked by religious rituals for Christians. Very shortly after birth, children were baptized, preferably by a priest but in emergency situations also by a midwife. Most weddings in Europe were conducted by a priest, who often blessed the marital bed (sometimes with the couple in it) later that day. Women who had given birth went through the ritual of churching forty days after the childbirth, in which they thanked God for their safe delivery, and were welcomed back into the congregation. There were rituals for the dying, and after death there were funerary rituals and memorial prayers and masses.

Pilgrims ask for healing at the tomb of Saint Sebastian in this oil painting from the late fifteenth century. Christians often regarded certain saints as specialists for particular types of requests, such as healing leprosy or giving birth to a healthy child, and their tombs and chapels became popular pilgrimage sites.

Along with holidays marking the year and sacraments and rituals marking the life cycle were a host of other religious activities. People participated in processions dedicated to the Virgin Mary or a specific saint to ask for a good harvest or prosperity in their city. They learned from their priests that good works as well as faith were necessary to get into heaven, so they attended church, gave money for the poor, prayed before eating and sleeping, and went on pilgrimages to sacred places. They paid church taxes and made donations for the building and maintenance of churches and cathedrals.

At least once a year, and sometimes much more regularly, people confessed their sins to the village priest, who then set certain actions, such as praying or fasting, as penance for those sins. Earthly penance was one of the seven sacraments, but was often not enough to make up for all sins, so penance continued after death (for those on their way to heaven) in purgatory, where souls waited before they were united with God. Such penance might be lessened or eliminated through the granting of indulgences, which were certificates issued by the church that remitted the penance owed to God because of sin. At first indulgences were granted to those who had done something spiritually meritorious, such as going on a Crusade or making a pilgrimage, but by the fifteenth century they were simply sold.

Christianity was not simply a set of religious practices, but also a powerful institution headed by the pope in Rome and a strong centralized bureaucracy. Key to this bureaucracy was a system of uniform church (or canon) law and church courts, which by the fifteenth century had jurisdiction over many aspects of life, including marriage and morality. Christianity was divided into territories (dioceses) headed by bishops, who generally came from wealthy families. Each diocese was divided into parishes, which were to be staffed by parish priests who were supposed to have received enough education to carry out religious services. Along with parishes, the western Christian church also maintained thousands of monasteries and convents, where individuals lived communally under the leadership of an abbot or abbess. Monks and nuns took religious vows of poverty, chastity, and obedience, and lived according to a monastic rule, which regulated the pattern of work, prayer, and other devotional activities during each day. Friars, such as the Dominicans, Franciscans, and Augustinians, were similar to monks and nuns in that they took special vows, but they lived out in the world rather than in cloistered houses. Taken all together, the various institutions of the Christian church owned about one quarter of the land in Europe and held political authority in many places. The pope ruled the papal states of central Italy, bishops governed cities and often large states, and monasteries had authority over villages and peasants.

Religious devotion was a central aspect of people's lives, but there was also dissatisfaction with the church. Many thought the pope and bishops had too much power. People complained that bishops did not live in their dioceses and did not supervise priests very well; that monks and friars were greedy and immoral, wheedling money out of people, maintaining concubines, and living too well; and that priests just mumbled the mass in Latin without understanding what the words meant. There were attempts to reform the church in the fourteenth and fifteenth centuries, but these remained limited in geographic scope and had little effect on the central hierarchy.

Criticism of the church grew louder in the early sixteenth century, and was voiced by some of Europe's most prominent scholars, including Desiderius Erasmus. It was also voiced by relative unknowns, such as Martin Luther, an Augustinian friar and professor of theology at the new university of Wittenberg in Germany. Luther was a nobody, from a third-rate university far from Europe's intellectual or cultural centers, so the church hierarchy did not worry much about him when he began to speak and write against certain practices. They should have. Initially Luther, like Erasmus, advocated reform, but by the early 1520s, he was calling for a break from the Catholic Church rather than change from within, and others were as well. He and his followers called their movement "evangelical," from the Greek word euangelion *meaning "gospel" or "good news." Later the movement that Luther started came to be known as the Protestant Reformation after a 1529 document issued by German princes protesting an order that they give up their religious innovations.*

Luther and other early Protestants agreed on many things. They thought that the pope's supreme authority in the church was not based on the Bible, that the church should give up much of its wealth, and that the prayers of priests or monks were no more powerful than those of ordinary Christians. They thought that religious services and the Bible should be in the languages people spoke, instead of Latin, which was restricted to a learned elite. They believed that no one should take special vows or live in monasteries, but that men and women should get married and live in families, serving God through their work. People should go to church and pray, but pray directly to God or Jesus, not to the Virgin Mary or the saints, who might have been good people but had no special powers or claim to holiness. They rejected the whole system of sacraments that the Catholic Church had developed, and saw only two—baptism and the Eucharist—as truly conveying God's grace. Protestants did not agree on everything, however, and Protestantism did not become a single church the way that Catholicism was, but splintered into many groups.

The Protestant reformers spread their criticisms and ideas through preaching, and also made skillful use of the new technology of the printing press with movable metal type, which had been invented in Germany in the 1450s. Many printed works included woodcuts and other illustrations, so that even those who could not read could grasp the main ideas. Many people found Protestant teachings appealing for a variety of reasons. City dwellers supported the idea that the church should not have special privileges. In the countryside, peasants liked the emphasis on the Bible and the idea that the clergy were no better than anyone else. Protestant ideas were attractive to political leaders, who broke with the papacy and the Roman church and established their own churches, with bishops and priests who received a salary from the state. Through a complex process that involved intellectual debate, preaching, political decisions, and war, by the middle of the sixteenth century, most of central and northern Europe had split from the Catholic Church.

The Catholic Church was slow in its response to this crisis, but by the later 1530s was beginning a drive for internal reform linked to earlier reform efforts and a counter-Reformation that opposed Protestants intellectually, institutionally, politically, and militarily. In this Catholic Reformation, the popes improved education for the clergy, tried to enforce moral standards among them, and supported the establishment of new religious orders such as the Jesuits that preached to the common people. Their own lives were models of decorum and piety, in contrast to the fifteenth- and early sixteenth-century popes who had concentrated on decorating churches and palaces and on enhancing the power of their own families. The reforming popes also established institutions that enforced religious conformity, such as the Inquisition and the Papal Index of Forbidden Books. By the end of the sixteenth century, the reinvigorated Catholic Church had been successful in halting Protestant advances in Europe, and had taken Catholicism around the world.

The religious reform that Luther started permanently changed the world in ways he never intended. Western Europe remained religiously divided from that point on, and the divisions were carried to the rest of the world by missionaries and colonists.

Popular Devotion

For most people in the fifteenth century, there was little separation between aspects of life regarded as sacred and those viewed as secular; religion permeated daily life. In the 1470s, for example, the English village official Robert Reynes recorded things he found interesting in a handwritten book. Along with comments about his family and village are many prayers, sayings, and cures, including a multipurpose protective charm involving nails, designed to remind believers of the nails used in Jesus's crucifixion.

Pope Innocent [VIII?] has granted seven gifts to every man who carries with him the length of three nails of our Lord Jesus Christ and worships them daily with five Our Fathers and five Hail Marys and the Creed: the first, he shall not die a sudden death; the second, he shall not be slain by a sword or knife; the third, his enemies shall not overcome him; the fourth, he shall have sufficient goods and an honest living; the fifth, poison or false witness will never harm him; the sixth, he shall not die without the sacraments of the church; the seventh, he shall be defended from all wicked spirits, fevers, pestilences, and all evil things.

Many people went on pilgrimages to churches or shrines, where they viewed religious relics regarded as holy, to express their piety and ask for the protection and assistance of saints. The English cathedral at Durham had hundreds of relics, and so many pilgrims visited that guards were needed for crowd control. A multipage inventory made in the late fourteenth century lists the cathedral's relics, which included material from biblical figures, saints from the early church, and more local holy figures. Viewing relics allowed people to share in the merits of the saints and martyrs that they represented, so wealthier people often had private relic collections as well.

Next, one small gilded and jeweled silver cross containing a piece of the Lord's Cross. Next, a piece from the Lord's manger in a blue silk purse. Next, four saints' bones in a small silver cross. Next, a piece of St. Godric's beard. Next, a little wooden box with some of the wood with which St. Lawrence was beaten and some tiny bones from the martyr St. Concordius, and pieces from St. Bernard the abbot's rib and from his hair, and a joint of St. Lawrence, partly burned by fire, in a crystal vial decorated with silver . . .

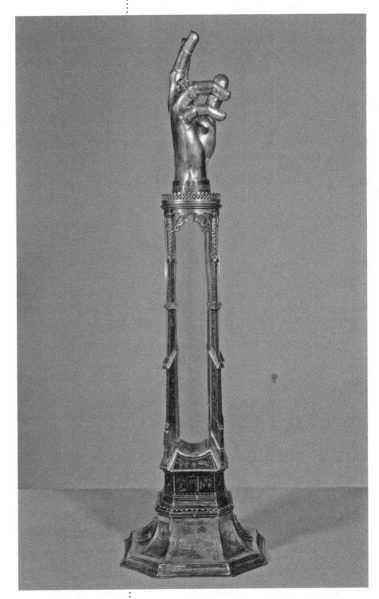

This reliquary made in 1337 of silver, rock crystal, and goldwork houses bones believed to be those from the arm of Saint Louis of Toulouse. Although many relics, such as milk from the Virgin Mary or pieces of Jesus's cross, were probably not what they purported to be, these might actually be Saint Louis's bones, because he was the brother of the·man for whom this reliquary was made, Robert d'Anjou, King of Naples. Louis had been made a bishop at the age of twenty-two, and after he died a year later his brother put pressure on various popes to have him made a saint, arguing that he had been especially devoted to the poor.

Pyx
Container consecrated by a priest

Next, a crystal pyx containing milk of the Blessed Virgin Mary. Next, a piece from the Blessed Virgin Mary's tomb and from her dress, and from the comb and wimple of her mother Anne in a crystal vial with silver feet. Next, a black vial with the tooth of St. Stephen and pieces of his skull and bones. Next, in a purse with red piping, a stone from the Lord's sepulcher, a stone from the church of Bethlehem, a stone from the sepulcher on Mount Sinai.

The Power of the Pope

Christianity was a matter of daily practice, and it was also a wealthy and powerful institution. In central and western Europe in the fifteenth century, Christianity was a hierarchy headed by the pope, who claimed spiritual authority over all Christians. Papal authority rested in theory on statements in the New Testament that were understood to give special powers to the apostle Peter, who was regarded as the first pope. In 1302, Pope Boniface VIII had forcefully laid out the idea of papal supreme power in the bull (or official statement) *Unam Sanctam*.

We [the pope uses the plural to refer to himself] are obliged by faith to believe and hold—and we do firmly believe and sincerely confess— that there is one holy, catholic and apostolic church, and that outside this church there is neither salvation nor remission of sins. . . . Of this one and only church there is one body and one head—not two heads, like a monster—namely Christ, and Christ's vicar is Peter and Peter's successor, for the Lord said to Peter himself, "feed my sheep." "My sheep" he said in general, not these or those sheep; wherefore he is understood to have committed them all to him. For this authority, although given to a man and exercised by a man, is not human, but rather divine, given at God's mouth to Peter and established on a rock for him and his successors in him whom he confessed, the Lord saying to Peter himself, "Whatsoever thou shalt bind," etc. Whoever therefore resists this power thus ordained of God, resists the ordinance of God . . . Furthermore we declare, state, define and pronounce that it is altogether necessary to salvation for every human creature to be subject to the Roman pontiff.

Calls for Reform

Papal claims to power were increasingly challenged in the fourteenth and fifteenth centuries by individuals and groups in different parts of Europe. Critics also accused church officials of greed and corruption, and of leading people to believe that donations alone, without faith, would get them into heaven. They called for reform. These calls became louder in the early sixteenth century, especially among Christian humanists such as Desiderius Erasmus, the most famous scholar of his time in all of Europe. Erasmus regarded humanist learning as a way to bring about reform of the church and a deepening of people's spiritual lives. In both serious works and in satires, Erasmus advocated for better education for both clergy and laity, hoping that people might be convinced to spend their time on prayer instead of pilgrimages, and their money on helping the needy instead of buying indulgences. His most popular work, *The Praise of Folly*, first published in 1511, was a witty satire poking fun at political, social, and especially religious institutions. Folly is a demi-goddess—like Justice—and the main text is her speech arguing that everything in life comes from her, that is, from people's foolishness, not their wisdom. Folly describes papal claims to power as an example of such foolishness, and offers a scathing account of the laziness and greed of current popes when compared with Christ and the early leaders of the church. Despite his harsh criticism, however, Erasmus never broke with the Catholic Church, but instead wanted reforms within the existing church structure.

Albrecht Dürer's engraving of Erasmus from 1526 shows him as an ideal humanist scholar, hard at work with pen in one hand and inkpot in the other, surrounded by books. The Latin and Greek inscription above him prominently displays Dürer's name and monogram. The engraving was made shortly after Erasmus's new Latin and Greek edition of the New Testament was published.

As to these Supreme Pontiffs who take the place of Christ . . . scarcely any kind of men live more softly or less oppressed with care; believing that they are amply acceptable to Christ if with a mystical and almost theatrical finery, with ceremonies, and with those titles of Beatitude and Reverence and Holiness, along with blessing and cursing, they perform the office of bishops. To work miracles is primitive and old-fashioned, hardly suited to our times; to instruct the people is irksome; to interpret the Holy Scriptures is pedantry; to pray is otiose; to shed tears is distressing and womanish; to live in poverty is sordid; to be beaten in war is dishonorable and less than worthy of one who will hardly admit kings, however great, to kiss his sacred foot; and finally, to die is unpleasant, to die on the cross a disgrace . . . .

Although this saying of Peter's stands in the Gospel, "We have left all and followed Thee," yet they give the name of his patrimony to lands, towns, tribute, imposts, and moneys. On behalf of these things, inflamed by zeal for Christ, they fight with fire and sword, not without shedding of Christian blood; and then they believe they defended the bride of Christ in apostolic fashion, having scattered what they are pleased to designate as "her enemies." As if the church had any enemies more pestilential than impious pontiffs who by their silence allow Christ to be forgotten, who enchain Him by mercenary rules, adulterate his teachings by forced interpretations, and crucify Him afresh by their scandalous life.

The popes and most church officials of the early sixteenth century paid no attention to mounting criticism, for their concerns were primarily political and financial. Pope Leo X, for example, a member of the Medici family, was constructing family chapels and tombs (for which he hired Michelangelo) and continuing the building of St. Peter's Basilica in Rome. He needed money for these, and in a papal bull, authorized a special St. Peter's indulgence, offering remission of all sins for those who purchased one. Archbishop Albert of Mainz in Germany also needed money for his efforts to become the bishop of several additional dioceses, and convinced Leo to allow him to keep a portion of the revenue from any indulgences sold in his territory. In 1515, Albert instructed his indulgence peddlers to travel widely and gave them written advice about how to make these indulgences attractive.

The following are the four principal gifts of grace that have been granted by the apostolic bull: any one of them can be had separately. It is on these four graces that the preachers must concentrate their utmost diligence, infiltrating them one by one into the ears of the faithful in the most effective way, and explaining them with all the ability they have.

The first principal grace is the plenary remission of all sins—the greatest of all graces, for the reason that man, a sinner who is deprived of divine grace, obtains through it perfect remission and God's grace anew.

A German single-page pamphlet shows a monk offering an indulgence, with the official seals of the pope attached, as people run to put their money in the box in exchange for his promise of heavenly bliss, symbolized by the dove above his head. Indulgences were sold widely in Germany, and became the first Catholic practice that Luther criticized openly. This pamphlet also attacks the sale of indulgences, calling this devilish and deceitful, a point of view expressed in the woodcut by the peddler's riding on a donkey, an animal that had long been used as a symbol of ignorance.

In addition, through this remission of sins, punishments to be undergone in purgatory because of offense done to the divine majesty, are remitted in full, and the punishments of the said purgatory are totally wiped out . . . Let every penitent who has made oral confession visit at least seven of the churches appointed for this purpose. . . .

If anyone for any reason seeks to be excused the visit to the said churches or altars, the penitentiaries, having heard the reason, may allow it: such a visit may be compounded by a larger financial contribution. This money must be placed in a box. . . .

The fourth principal grace is the plenary remission of all sins for the souls that exist in purgatory, which the pope grants and concedes by means of intercessions, so that a contribution placed by the living in the repository on their behalf counts as one which a man might make or give for himself. . . . There is no need for the contributors to be of contrite heart or to make oral confession, since this grace depends (as the bull makes clear) on the love in which the departed died and the contributions which the living pay.

Albert's diocese included the city of Wittenberg, where Martin Luther was a friar and university professor. Luther was disturbed by what seemed to him a combination of the worst of both institutional corruption and misguided popular beliefs. In 1519, he wrote a letter to Archbishop Albert, laying out his ideas as ninety-five theses, or scholarly points of argument, against the indulgence sale. In this he does not dispute the idea of indulgences as such, just the extent to which they were being sold, and comments that surely the pope would not support this.

5.   The pope neither desires nor is able to remit any penalties except those imposed by his own authority or that of the canons.

27.   They preach only human doctrines who say that as soon as the money clinks into the money chest, the soul flies out of purgatory.

32.   Those who believe that they can be certain of their salvation because they have indulgence letters will be eternally damned, together with their teachers.

41.   Papal indulgences must be preached with caution, lest people erroneously think that they are preferable to other good works of love.

43.   Christians are to be taught that he who gives to the poor or lends to the needy does a better deed than he who buys an indulgence.

The Posting of the 95 Theses
Luther wrote his arguments against indulgences as a numbered series of theses, or points of disputation. In this he was following a long tradition among scholars, who argued theological and philosophical issues in this way. Later biographies of Luther reported that he also nailed these theses to the door of the Wittenberg castle church on October 31, 1517, the day before All Saints' Day, when church attendance would be high. Such an act would have been strange—they were in Latin and written for those learned in theology, not normal church-goers—but it has become a standard part of Luther lore. Whether this actually happened or not is impossible to know for sure, but there is no doubt that Luther's theses were quickly published, both in Latin and in German translation, and sparked a revolt against the Catholic Church far greater than Luther had imagined.

This illustration from a 1526 Catholic book entitled *The Catalog of Heretics* shows a "column of heresy," with Luther on the top; the list of books classified as heretical in this book became the basis for the later Papal Index of Forbidden Books. In the woodcut, one demon blows ideas into Luther's ear with a bellows, as another drags him with a chain into the flames of hell. Catholics and Protestants both used harsh images in their campaigns against one another.

50. Christians are to be taught that if the pope knew the exactions of the indulgence-preachers, he would rather that the basilica of St. Peter were burned to ashes than built up with the skin, flesh, and bones of his sheep.

Reform Becomes Reformation

Even though the 95 Theses had not criticized the pope directly, Luther was ordered to recant and come to Rome, but he did neither. He continued to develop his own ideas, and gradually decided that the church would not be able to reform itself, and so called for a break from the Catholic Church. Like many Renaissance humanists had with literature, he sought to strip away what he saw as medieval corruptions to Christianity and return to purer original forms. Luther was greatly troubled by doubts about his own worth and sinfulness, and in reflection on the Bible found the basis of an understanding of essential Christian doctrines different from the one he had been taught. In 1520, he summarized his beliefs in *The Freedom of a Christian* and here put particular emphasis on faith as a gift of God.

First, let us consider the inner man to see how a righteous, free, and pious Christian, that is, a spiritual, new, and inner man, becomes what he is. It is evident that no external thing has any influence in producing Christian righteousness or freedom, or in producing unrighteousness or servitude.... One thing, and only one thing, is necessary for Christian life, righteousness, and freedom. That one thing is the most holy Word of God, the gospel of Christ....

You may ask, "What then is the Word of God, and how shall it be used, since there are so many words of God?" I answer: The Apostle explains this in Romans 1. The Word is the gospel of God concerning his Son, who was made flesh, suffered, rose from the dead, and was glorified through the Spirit who sanctifies ... Again, in Rom. 1 [:17], "he who through faith is righteous shall live." The Word of God cannot be received and cherished by any works whatever but only by faith. Therefore it is clear that, as the soul needs only the Word of God for its life and righteousness, so it is justified by faith alone and not any works; for if it could be justified by anything else, it would not need the Word, and consequently it would not need faith.

Luther was not alone in rejecting key doctrines of the church. In Switzerland, Ulrich Zwingli, the priest at Zurich's major church, also preached against indulgences and the emphasis on good works. In his sermons and writings, he agreed with Luther about the primacy of faith and Scripture, as he comments in *Of the Clarity and Certainty of the Word of God*, published in 1522. Also like Luther, Zwingli called for a split from the Catholic Church. Many others agreed, and during the 1520s sections of Germany, Switzerland, and other parts of central and northern Europe broke with the church in what was later termed the Protestant Reformation. Luther and Zwingli, and their followers, agreed on many things, but they did not agree on exactly how to understand the ritual of the Eucharist (also called communion, the Lord's Supper, and in Catholicism, the Mass). Because of this, the Protestant Reformation split into two wings: those who followed Luther, often called "Evangelical," and those who followed Zwingli (and later John Calvin), called "Reformed." In general, Zwinglian Reformed ideas spread more widely in Switzerland and south Germany, and Lutheran Evangelical ideas were more popular in northern Germany and Scandinavia.

In my youth I devoted myself as much to human learning as did others of my age. Then, some seven or eight years ago, I undertook to devoting myself entirely to the Scriptures, and the conflicting philosophy and theology of the schoolmen constantly presented difficulties. But eventually I came to a conclusion—led thereto by the Scriptures and the Word of God—and decided "You must drop all that and learn God's will directly from his own word." . . .

Finally here is the answer to any opposition. It is my conviction that the word of God must be held by us in the highest esteem (the Word of God being that alone which comes from God's Spirit) and no such credence is to be given to any other word. It is certain and cannot fail us; it is clear and does not let us wander in darkness. It teaches itself, it explains itself and brings the light of full salvation and grace to the human soul . . . The words are clear: God's teaching clearly enlightens, teaches and gives certainty without any intervention on the part of human knowledge.

Protestant ideas spread to England, but in that country the actual break with the Catholic Church resulted primarily from King Henry VIII's desire for an heir. The king was initially opposed to Lutheran teachings, but his first marriage had produced only one daughter, Mary, and in 1525 he wanted an annulment so that he could marry again. Normally arranging an annulment with the pope would not have been a problem, but at that point Pope Clement VII was essentially the prisoner of the German Emperor Charles V. Charles was the nephew of Henry's wife Catherine of Aragon and thus was vigorously opposed to an annulment. So the pope stalled, and Henry gradually took over control of the English church. He obtained an annulment from the highest official in his new Church

Music and the Reformation

Some reformers, including Zwingli, objected to music in the church as distracting, but others saw music, especially congregational hymn singing, as a way to teach people. Martin Luther himself wrote many hymns. Some of these attacked the Catholic Church:

> Lord, keep us steadfast in thy Word,
> And curb the pope's and Turk's vile sword,
> Who seek to topple from the throne,
> Jesus Christ, thine only Son.

Others conveyed ideas that all Christians shared:

> A mighty fortress is our God,
> A sword and shield victorious.

Divorced, Beheaded, Died

Henry VIII ultimately had six wives. As with any monarch, his choices in spouses reflected politics as much as personal preference. Catherine of Aragon, his first wife, was the daughter of Ferdinand and Isabella of Spain, Europe's most powerful rulers. Anne Boleyn, his second wife, did catch the royal eye, but she was also from a prominent noble family. After Anne did not give Henry the son he wanted, he had her executed as punishment for trumped-up charges of witchcraft, adultery, incest, and treason. As an eyewitness reported, "She kneeled down on both her knees, and said, To Jesus Christ I commend my soul and with that word suddenly the hangman of Calais smote off her head at one stroke with a sword: her body with the head was buried in the choir of the Chapel in the Tower." Jane Seymour, Henry's third wife, was from another important noble family. She quickly became pregnant, at which, as a contemporary reported, "all gave laud and praise to God for joy about it . . . and various great fires were made in London, with a barrel of wine at every fire for the poor people to drink as long as it lasted." Jane Seymour died twelve days after giving birth to Henry's long-awaited son, and Henry next married Anne of Cleves, a German princess, to help cement his alliances with continental Protestants. Henry immediately disliked her, and arranged to have the marriage annulled; Anne agreed (perhaps the negative feelings were mutual), and was given a castle to live in. Less than a month later Henry married Catherine Howard, an English noblewoman thirty years his junior from a Catholic family, who hoped they might use her to bring Catholicism back to England. Instead she flirted with men at court, several of whom might have been her lovers before her marriage, and Henry also charged her with adultery and treason. Like her cousin Anne Boleyn, Catherine Howard was executed. Next Henry married Catherine Parr, who herself had already been widowed twice and was known to be a good Protestant. She reconciled his two daughters to him, and outlived him.

of England, and married a court lady, Anne Boleyn, who (to Henry's great disappointment) gave birth to another daughter, Elizabeth. Working through Parliament, in 1534 he ordered everyone holding office in England to sign an oath agreeing with his measures. Almost all officials did sign, and England slowly became a Protestant country. Monasteries were closed, priests married, church services were in English, and the monarchy took over church land.

Be it enacted by authority of this present Parliament, that the King our sovereign lord, his heirs and successors, Kings of this realm, shall be taken, accepted, and reputed the only supreme head on earth of the Church of England, called Angelicana Ecclesia, and shall have and enjoy, annexed and united to the imperial crown of this realm, as well the style and title thereof, as all honors, dignities, preeminences, jurisdictions, privileges, authorities, immunities, profits, and commodities, to the said dignity of supreme head of the same Church belonging and appertaining; and that our said sovereign lord, his heirs and successors, Kings of this realm, shall have full power and authority from time to time to visit, repress, redress, reform, order, correct, restrain, and amend all such errors, heresies, abuses, offenses, contempts, and enormities, whatsoever they be.

The Catholic Response

At first the Catholic Church reacted rather fitfully to Protestant challenges. On hearing about what was happening in Germany, in 1520 Pope Leo X issued a papal bull declaring Luther's teachings to be heresy. Luther burned the bull, along with books of canon law. Leo then excommunicated him, but the pope was more worried about attacks on papal territories by the Ottoman Turks and fighting in Italy between troops of the German emperor and the French king than by what he interpreted as a dispute among theologians, so he never went any further against Luther.

Arise O Lord and judge thy cause. . . . Arise O Peter, and in the name of the pastoral charge committed to thee from on high, put forth thy strength in the cause of the holy Roman Church, the mother of all churches, the mistress of the faith. . . . In a word, let every saint arise and the whole remaining universal church. . . . Let intercession be made to almighty God, that his sheep may be purged of their errors and every heresy be expelled from the confines of the faithful, and that God may deign to preserve the peace and unity of his holy church.

Leo and his successor Clement VII (pontificate 1523–1534) were both members of the wealthy and powerful Medici family, living examples of the problems people saw in the Catholic Church: They lived lavishly, were much more concerned with art and politics than with spiritual matters, held multiple offices at the same time, and used their positions to reward family members. They were completely uninterested in reforming the church, but beginning in 1534 with Pope Paul III, the papal court became the center of the reform movement within the Catholic Church, later called the Catholic Reformation. Paul appointed reform-minded cardinals, and in 1537 asked two of them to make a thorough report on the state of the church. They reported appalling problems.

Concerning ordination [of priests]: no care is taken. Whoever they are (uneducated, of appalling morals, under age), they are routinely admitted to holy orders . . . Reverence for divine service is so much diminished as now to be virtually extinct. . . . Your Holiness should order every bishop to take the greatest care in this and, observing the laws, appoint a professor to instruct their clergy in letters and in morals . . . .

Concerning the government of the Christian faithful, the most fundamental abuse in need of reformation is that bishops and priests must not be absent from their churches, but must be resident for they are entrusted with their care. What sight can be more piteous than deserted churches? Almost all the shepherds have deserted their flocks or abandoned them to hirelings. A heavy penalty must be imposed, not only censures but the withholding of income . . . [on all] absent for more than three Sundays per year . . .

Concerning Rome: honest manners should flourish in this city and church, mother and teacher of other churches . . . [yet] whores perambulate like matrons or ride on muleback, with whom noblemen, cardinals and priests consort in broad daylight.

Paul III and his successors worked to reform these abuses, and also sought to combat the spread of Protestant teaching. In 1542, Paul III issued a papal bull establishing the Roman Inquisition, which investigated those suspected of heresy.

From the beginning of our assumption of the apostolic office we have been concerned for the flourishing of the Catholic faith and the purging of heresy. Those seduced by diabolical wiles should then return to the fold and unity of the church. Those who persist in their damnable course should be removed and their punishment serve as an example to others. Nevertheless we hope that the mercy of God, the prayers of the faithful and the preaching of the learned would cause them to recognize their errors and come back to the holy Catholic Church . . . [Therefore] we have appointed

Hanno the Elephant
Pope Leo X loved magnificence and display, and was interested in the exotic. As a gift for his coronation, King Manuel of Portugal sent him a white Indian elephant, which the Pope named Hanno after a great Carthaginian general. When the elephant died several years later, the pope asked Raphael to paint its portrait, which later artists frequently copied, as in this sketch. Pope Leo had the animal buried in the papal palace and wrote a flowery epitaph: "The Roman people marveled, and in my brutish breast they perceived human feelings. Fate envied me my residence in the blessed papal palace. And had not the patience to let me serve my master a full three years. But I wish, oh gods, that the time which Nature would have assigned to me, and Destiny stole away, You will add to the life of the great Leo." The pope's fondness for the animal and his extravagant expenditures on it were criticized by reformers and mocked by satirists, and Hanno became a symbol of what was wrong with the papacy.

As religious disagreements grew sharper, both Protestants and Catholics prepared for war. Here armed French Catholics, including priests and monks with helmets, shields, and weapons, march out of a gate in Paris.

our beloved son, Giovanni Pietro Carafa, Inquisitor General with jurisdiction throughout Christendom including Italy and the Roman Curia ... [He and his subordinates] are to investigate by way of inquisition all and every who wander from the way of the Lord and the catholic faith, as well as those suspected of heresy, together with their followers and abettors, public or private, direct or indirect. The guilty and the suspects are to be imprisoned and proceeded against up to the final sentence. Those judged guilty are to be punished in accord with canonical penalties. After the infliction of death their property may be sold. The aid of the civil arm may be invoked to implement whatever measures are deemed necessary. Anyone who dares to impede this will incur the anger of almighty God and the blessed apostles, Peter and Paul.

Reforms involved religious orders as well as the papacy. Older religious orders carried out measures to get back to their original aims, and new religious orders were founded. The most important of the new religious orders was the Society of Jesus or the Jesuits, founded by Ignatius Loyola in 1534. Loyola was a Spanish nobleman who decided to give up his life as a soldier, and instead devote himself to the pope and the Catholic Church. Loyola attracted energetic young men to the Jesuits, who saw their calling as education and conversion. Jesuits founded schools, taught at universities, and preached popular sermons. In Europe, they became very effective at stopping the further spread of Protestant ideas, and even reconverted some areas to Catholicism. Jesuit missionaries worked to convert local people to Christianity in places far beyond Europe, including New Spain, Brazil, India, China, and Japan. In all of his writings, Loyola defended the traditional doctrines of the church, and urged his followers to do so as well, as in his "Rules for Thinking with the Church," a set of guidelines that were written in the 1530s and first published in 1541.

We must put aside all judgment of our own, and keep the mind ever ready and prompt to obey in all things the true Spouse of Christ our Lord, our holy Mother, the hierarchical Church ...

We must praise highly religious life, virginity, and [sexual] continence; and matrimony ought not to be praised as much as any of these.

We should praise vows of religion, obedience, poverty, chastity, and vows to perform other works conducive to perfection ...

We should show our esteem for the relics of the saints by venerating them and praying to the saints ...

In Christ our Lord, the bridegroom, and in His spouse the Church, only one Spirit holds sway, which governs and rules for the salvation of souls.

Jesuit missionaries traveled to Japan, where they converted local men and women, who then persuaded others to accept Christianity. By 1580 there were more than 100,000 Christians in Japan. A few Japanese converts returned to Europe with Jesuit priests, where they were regarded as curiosities and celebrities, as in this 1586 German newspaper, reporting on a visit of four Japanese to the city of Milan.

CHAPTER 7

Radical Hopes, Popular Protests, and Mystical Visions

Peasants celebrate a wedding in this 1568 painting by Pieter Brueghel, a Dutch painter known for his depictions of common people. Festivities such as this offered an occasional break from the grueling work of village life, where inequalities between rich and poor made the teachings of the radical reformers about a more equitable distribution of wealth attractive to many people.

Protestant ideas alone did not bring about the Reformation. What made the reform started by Luther different from earlier reform movements was the fact that many political leaders accepted these ideas, broke with the papacy and the Roman Catholic Church, and established their own local churches. Individuals might have been convinced of the truth of Protestant teachings by hearing sermons, listening to hymns, or reading pamphlets, but territories became Protestant when their ruler, whether a king, a duke, or a city council, brought in a reformer or two to reeducate the territory's clergy, sponsored public sermons, confiscated church property, and closed convents and monasteries. The religion of a region ultimately came to depend primarily on the ruler's preference. Rulers' motivations were mixed and varied; spiritual aims blended with desires to end the economic and political power of the papacy in their territories, gain the income from church lands, oppose neighboring states that remained Catholic, and expand authority over more aspects of their subjects' lives.

Kirchen
Ozdnũg/ In meiner gnedigen herrn der Marggrauen zu Bran denburg/ vnd eins Erberen Rats der Stat Nürnberg Oberkeyt vñ gepieten/ Wie man sich Bayde mit der Leer vnd Ceremonien halten solle

M. D. XXXIII.

The 1533 church ordinance issued by the newly Protestant margrave of Brandenburg and the Protestant city council of Nuremberg spelled out, as the title page indicates, "how both the teachings and ceremonies are to be carried out" in a properly Protestant fashion. Similar church ordinances were issued and published in most areas that became Protestant.

Luther's own ruler, the Elector of Saxony, was an early convert, and the political situation in Germany is the primary reason that Luther was not arrested. Germany was not a unified country ruled by a king or queen like France or England, but an empire divided into many smaller territories, loosely presided over by an emperor who was elected by a small group of nobles. The ruler of the territory where Luther lived was one of these nobles. Emperor Charles V outlawed Luther and remained a firm supporter of the Catholic Church, but he was not willing to order soldiers into Saxony. Other leaders of territories within the empire followed the elector's example and accepted Protestant ideas, fully understanding the practical benefits. The kings of Denmark and Sweden did as well, as did the ruling council of Scotland, and these countries joined England and many German territories as Protestant states.

Whether rulers became Protestant or remained Catholic, they expected that everyone in their territory would follow their example. Most people agreed with their rulers that church and state needed to be united, but some rejected this and sought to create a voluntary community of believers as they understood it to have existed in New Testament times. In terms of theology and spiritual practices, these individuals and groups varied widely, although historians generally term them "radicals" for their insistence on a more extensive break with the past. Many of them rejected infant baptism, for they thought that belief should precede baptism. Some adopted the baptism of adult believers—for which they were given the title of "Anabaptists" or rebaptizers by their enemies—whereas others saw all outward sacraments or rituals, including baptism, as misguided and concentrated on inner spiritual transformation.

Both Protestant and Catholic authorities regarded the radicals' ideas about a voluntary church as dangerous, and threatened them with prison or other punishments, including execution. Persecution led radical leaders and their followers to flee to areas in Europe that were more tolerant, including parts of eastern Europe. Some of them, such as the Hutterites and Mennonites, eventually came to North America, where they maintain their beliefs and communities today. Many other religious groups, including the Quakers, Unitarians, and Baptists, have their roots in the radical Reformation. The radicals' notion that religious allegiance should be voluntary and that church and state should be separate later became part of the U.S. Constitution.

Radicals were not the only people who met with violence. Both Catholic and Protestant rulers often forbade people from Christian *groups other than their own to worship, and sometimes arrested and killed them. Catholic leaders imprisoned and executed Protestants, and Protestants imprisoned and executed Catholics and other types of Protestants. The suppression of ideas judged religiously deviant, and the use of violence to wipe them out, had not been unknown in western Europe before the sixteenth century, but the extent of both increased significantly. Religious rebellions and disputes became full-blown wars in different parts of Europe from the mid-1520s onward: Switzerland, Germany, France, and the Netherlands all saw battle. War plus religious persecution led to large numbers of refugees moving from place to place. Dutch, French, and German Protestants fled to England during the reign of Henry VIII and his son Edward VI, but were forced back to the Continent when Henry's daughter Mary, an ardent Catholic, took over the throne when Edward died. Catholics fled from Bohemia (now part of the Czech Republic) when that area became Protestant in the 1580s, but Protestants fled in turn when Bohemia became Catholic again several decades later. In the early seventeenth century, English Protestants who disagreed with the Protestant state church there moved to the Netherlands, where the form of Protestantism was more to their liking and the government was more tolerant of all religions. Some of these English Protestants were among the first immigrants to Britain's North American colonies, where they—ironically—often tried to enforce religious uniformity themselves, forcing those who disagreed to move. The first English settlements in what became Connecticut and Rhode Island were, in fact, started by refugees from Massachusetts.*

German peasants and some radicals sought to use religious ideas as a basis for changing the here-and-now, but other radicals, as well as many who remained within the Catholic Church and the Protestant mainstream, emphasized the inner life of the spirit more than the visible world. Since the earliest centuries of Christianity, some within the church had objected to its becoming a powerful hierarchy with complex theology. They thought that close relations with the divine should not be limited to an elite group with official positions or advanced learning, but could be achieved by many people through prayer, rituals, and sometimes mystical encounters such as seeing visions, hearing voices, or sensing God in ways that involved the body and emotions. Some mystics came to be revered as saints because people thought they had a special connection to God. At times certain mystics challenged church and political hierarchies, and officials had them arrested, imprisoned, or even killed. Other mystics lived quietly in monasteries, convents, or with their families, and did not view God's speaking to them as a reason to disobey authorities or try to change things.

Sometimes the tension between obedience to authorities and a more individualistic spirituality that is part of Christian history can be found within the writings of a single person. Teresa of Ávila, a Spanish nun who became the sixteenth century's most influential mystic and also one of the most important Catholic reformers and thinkers of all time, reflects that tension. In Teresa's descriptions of her mystical visions, she puts an emphasis on God's power and the freedom this brings to believers. Her language sounds much like that of Luther on these points, a reminder that although Protestant and Catholic reformers differed on many things, they also shared beliefs and ideas.

Church and State

Both Luther and the Swiss reformer Ulrich Zwingli worked closely with political authorities, viewing them as fully justified in asserting control over the church in their territories. In Luther's 1523 pamphlet *On Secular Authority*, he instructed all Christians to obey their secular rulers, whom he saw as divinely ordained to maintain order.

Seeing that Christians need neither the secular Sword nor law, why does Paul in Romans 13: [1] say to all Christians: "Let every soul be subject to power and superiority!" And St. Peter [1 Pet. 2:13]: "Be subject to every human ordinance etc." My answer is: I have already said that Christians among themselves and for themselves need no law and no Sword, for they have no use for them. But because a true Christian, while he is on the earth, lives for and serves his neighbor and not himself, he does things that are of no benefit to himself, but of which his neighbor stands in need. Such is the nature of the Christian's spirit. Now the Sword is indispensable for the whole world, to preserve peace, punish sin, and restrain the wicked. And therefore Christians readily submit themselves to be governed by the Sword, they pay taxes, honor those in authority, serve and help them, and do what they can to uphold their power, so that they may continue their work, and that honor and fear of authority may be maintained. . . . And therefore if you see that there is a lack of hangmen, court officials, judges, lords or princes, and you find that you have the necessary skills, then you should offer your services and seek office, so that authority, which is so greatly needed,

The coat of arms of King Christian III of Denmark and Norway appears as a frontispiece of a 1550 Bible in Danish. He invited Lutheran reformers from Wittenberg to his court and cities in the 1530s, and became the first ruler outside of Germany to accept the Protestant Reformation. His subjects largely followed his lead, a pattern that most people in the sixteenth century thought was essential for public order, for they assumed that the religion of the ruler and that of the ruled should be the same.

INSIGNIA CHRISTI.
ANI TERTII DANO.
RVM REGIS.&c.
ANNO.M.D.L.

VNICA
SPES MEA
CHRISTVS
C.R.D.

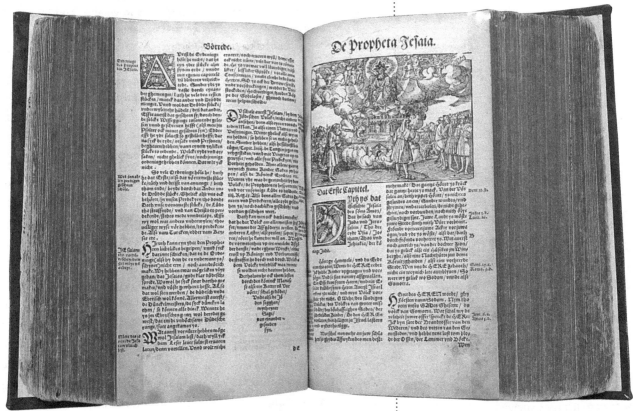

will never come to be held in contempt, become powerless, or perish. The world cannot get by without it.

Like Luther, Zwingli, and other Protestants, radical reformers grounded their ideas in the Bible. They often attempted to follow Christ's commandments as given in the Bible to the letter, arguing that he meant exactly what he said; thus they rejected infant baptism and swearing oaths, and were often pacifists. Michael Sattler, an early leader of a radical Anabaptist group, defended many of their beliefs with Biblical citations at his trial in 1527, as reported by his fellow believers in an account that was later printed as part of an Anabaptist martyrology.

As to baptism we say infant baptism is of no avail to salvation. For it is written [Rom. 1:17] that we live by faith alone. Again [Mark 16:16]: He that believeth and is baptized shall be saved . . . we hold that we are not to swear before the authorities [i.e., take an oath], for the Lord says [Matt. 5:34]: Swear not, but let your communication be, Yea, yea; nay, nay . . . If the Turks should come, we ought not to resist them. For it is written [Matt. 5:21]: Thou shalt not kill. We must not defend ourselves against the Turks and others of our persecutors, but are to beseech God with earnest prayer to repel and resist them.

Luther first translated the Bible into the type of German spoken in Saxony where he lived, known as High German, and later translated it into the slightly different type of German spoken in the far northern areas along the seacoast, known as Low German. This 1545 Bible is one of the few surviving copies in Low German. Every Protestant reformer, the radicals as well as those who worked with political authorities, supported translations of the Bible into the languages that people spoke.

Some radical groups opposed all differences in wealth, and owned all their property in common, a practice that appealed to peasants and poor townspeople, who often opposed hierarchies within the church, wanted the congregation to have a more active role, and expected the second coming of Christ—predicted in the Book of Revelation—to happen soon. The Hutterite leader Peter Walpot was one of many who found Biblical support for these ideas, as he wrote in *True Yieldedness and the Christian Community of Goods*, published in 1577.

No one may serve two masters (Matthew 6; Luke 16). For you will hate the one and love the other or obey the one and despise the other. You cannot serve God and Mammon—that is, earthly possessions and riches. For like a lock, the love of and concern for money occupies the heart. Therefore, you should not strive for surplus and then seek to justify it. For Christ said that it is impossible to serve and nurture both of these two masters. So don't say that it is possible! . . . Private property does not belong in the Christian church. Private property is a thing of the world, of the heathen, of those without divine love, of those who will have their own way. For there would be no property if it were not for selfish will. But the true community of goods belongs among believers. For by divine law all things should be held in common and nobody should take for himself what is God's any more than the air, rain, snow or water, the sun or other elements . . . Greed is a serious and evil sickness which blinds a person's eyes and stops up his ears. The disease of greed withers the hand so that it is useless in helping others. The greedy lose their reason and do not know what or why they are here on this earth. Greed allows neither the self, the conscience, nor the soul to know salvation.

Martyrs and Enemies

Catholics and most Protestants, including Luther, opposed the radicals' unwillingness to accept a state church and viewed their ideas as a potential threat to political stability and social order. Many thousands were persecuted, tortured, and executed, sometimes in very gruesome ways. In 1527, Catholic authorities found Michael Sattler guilty of heresy, and ordered his death, as the account of his execution records.

Michael Sattler shall be delivered to the executioner, who shall lead him to the place of execution and cut out his tongue, then forge him fast to a wagon and thereon with red-hot tongs twice tear pieces from his body; and after he has been brought outside the gate, he shall be plied five times more in the same manner.

Jeroen, together with his Wife,
From evil suffered sorrow great,
So they were not forsaken
By God, in their sad, dark affliction . . .

Jeroen to the rack was brought,
Much he suffered pain and torment,
The bishop's helper racked him long,
And while he lay there, bound up tight,
With water the bishop poured him full;
The cruel Wolves about him stood,
Expecting his need to make him speak . . . .

But then he turned his craft on Lijsken,
Thinking to make that woman recant;
But her pillar was the word of God,
And she endured, remained fast standing . . .

The Sophists and the Hypocrites,
So very much were angered,
That they could not tear to bits
God's children through their teachings false.
And so the Council did decide
That those dear lambs so sweet they would
Cast out, away, to their deaths.
That's how they quenched their cruel hearts!

Jeroen, going to the sacrifice,
Was very well prepared to die;
Big Hendrik, standing there as well,
Patiently waited for death with him.
They stepped together, the two of them,
Thus to the stake, and had no fear,
For their Father they did long,
To whom they did commend their Spirit.

Jeroen had to leave his love,
That was for him a sorrow great;
For she was fruitful with their child.
And when she had borne that child,
In torment, with great labour,
They threw that small sheep in the River
    Scheldt.
    —Anabaptist hymn memorializing the
    execution of a husband and wife in 1552

Radical reformers are burned at the stake in Strasbourg in 1528, in an engraving made during the sixteenth century and later published many times in collections of the stories of religious martyrdom. Both Catholics and Protestants tortured and executed radicals, often with horrific violence, fearing that their teachings would lead to social unrest or political revolts.

Sattler was not alone in his punishment, for the trial account notes that after he was eventually "burned to ashes as a heretic," the rest of his group was killed as well; the sympathetic perspective of the anonymous person writing this account comes through in the language chosen.

His fellow brethren were executed with the sword, and the sisters drowned. His wife, also after being subjected to many entreaties, admonitions, and threats, under which she remained steadfast, was drowned a few days afterward. Done the 21st day of May, A.D. 1527.

Sir Henry Sidney, Queen Elizabeth's Lord-deputy in Ireland, rides out from Dublin Castle with an armed force to put down rebellions. In this English woodcut, which included a poem praising Sidney and the queen, the severed heads of Irish leaders who opposed English measures in Ireland are posted on spikes above the gate.

Efforts to impose the religion of the ruler met with particular resistance in Ireland, ruled by England in the sixteenth century in many ways as a colony, with little say in its own laws or taxes. All landholders had to swear loyalty to the English monarch, which after the Reformation meant acknowledging that Henry or Elizabeth was the supreme head of the church. Some Irish converted, or at least swore the oath, but many refused, secretly attending Catholic services and supporting priests. Resistance to English domination led to several armed rebellions, which were brutally suppressed with the lands of the rebels turned over to English or Scottish

Protestant landholders. Catholicism became a central part of Irish national identity, as is already hinted at in this anonymous description of the Irish church, written in the late sixteenth century. Catholicism continued to play an important role in Irish identity, emerging later in the movement for Irish independence from Britain in the early twentieth century.

And the ruler of England and Ireland at this time is Queen Elizabeth . . . . And the English are saying that she is the supreme head of religion, and that is a lie, because we are certain that the pope is head of the holy Catholic church and what the English say is true in the sense that she is indeed supreme head of their own evil religion in her own dominions, for there is no fast or Lent or . . . holy day under their law, though God ordained their observance, nor is there honour or love of sacred buildings. And further, they are the greatest murderers and the proudest people in all Europe, and I am surprised that God tolerates them so long in power—except that he is long-suffering and that his avenging hand is slow but sure, and besides, that the Irish themselves are bad, and that this misfortune is to chastise and correct them.

This painting of the 1572 St. Bartholomew's Day Massacre in France, during which thousands of Protestants were killed, includes gruesome scenes drawn from published reports, such as blood overflowing from a canal, children's bodies dragged through the dirt, and women impaled on spits. The French Protestant artist who painted it put Catherine de Medici, the Catholic queen of France, in the middle of the slaughter, sword in hand. Visual propaganda as well as printed pamphlets increased religious hatred on all sides in the sixteenth century.

Religious differences were understood as matters of (eternal) life and death in the sixteenth century, and the Reformation was often accompanied by horrific violence. Protestant and Catholic mobs in France, for example, ransacked and burned houses, killed livestock, and murdered their opponents, often in grisly fashion. Printed pamphlets written in vivid language spread reports of these actions, further fanning the flames of hatred, as in this 1564 Protestant pamphlet. Both sides organized militias, and the conflict grew into a long series of religious wars.

[These] execrable executioners slit the throat of this mother, then shot her five times in the breasts with a pistol, and then burned the hands and feet of Faith, her eldest daughter . . . And after the massacre was completed and the house was ransacked, [the mob] led pigs in to the house and enclosed them there, in order to make them eat all those poor dead corpses.

The Peasants' War

Among the many violent events related to the Protestant Reformation was the German Peasants' War of 1524–1526. What began as a protest about fishing in a forbidden stream quickly became a widespread rebellion, the largest mass uprising in Europe before the French Revolution. Local groups of peasants formed regional revolutionary organizations and military alliances in southwestern and then central and southeastern Germany. In March 1525, a union of these groups issued the "Twelve Articles of Memmingen," a manifesto listing their grievances. Many of these were about taxes, labor services, duties, and rights. The Twelve Articles were published as a small, cheap pamphlet that was quickly reprinted many times. The peasants' demands were backed by military action, and peasant armies seized castles, noble houses, abbeys, and a few cities; in other cities townspeople themselves revolted, calling for civil rights and religious reform.

The Third Article: It has been the custom hitherto for men to hold us as their own property, which is pitiable enough, considering that Christ has delivered and redeemed us all, without exception, by the shedding of his precious blood, the lowly as well as the great. Accordingly, it is consistent with Scripture that we should be free and wish to be so. Not that we would wish to be absolutely free and under no authority. God does not teach us that we should lead a disorderly life in the lusts of the flesh, but that we should love the Lord our God and our neighbor. We would gladly observe all this as God has commanded us in celebration of the communion. He has not commanded us not to obey authorities, but rather that we should be humble, not only towards those in authority, but towards everyone. We are thus ready to yield obedience according to God's law to our elected and regular authorities in all proper things becoming to a Christian. We, therefore, take it for granted that you will release us from serfdom as true Christians, unless it should be shown us from the Gospel that we are serfs.

The Fourth Article: In the fourth place it has been the custom heretofore, that no poor man should be allowed to touch venison or

One of many pamphlets printed during the Peasants' War shows the wheel of fortune in the middle, with the pope strapped to it. His supporters are on one side, labeled "Romanists and Sophists" (a reference to ancient Greek philosophers who deceived people with clever arguments) and "peasants and good Christians" are on the other side. Although the little rhyme above the picture says "Now is the time of the wheel of fortune, and only God knows who will rise above," the author clearly favors the peasants.

wild fowl, or fish in flowing water, which seems to us quite unseemly and unbrotherly, as well as selfish and not agreeable to the word of God. In some places the authorities preserve the game to our great annoyance and loss, recklessly permitting unreasoning animals to destroy to no purpose our crops, which God suffers to grow for the use of man, and yet we remain quiet. This is neither godly nor neighborly. For when God created man he gave him dominion over all the animals, over the birds of the air and over the fish in the water. Accordingly it is our desire if a man holds possession of waters that he should prove from satisfactory documents that his right has been unwittingly acquired by purchase. We do not wish to take from him by force, but his rights should be exercised in a Christian and brotherly fashion. But whosoever cannot produce such evidence should surrender his claim with good grace.

The Fifth Article: In the fifth place we are aggrieved in the matter of woodcutting, for the noble folk have appropriated all the woods to themselves alone. If a poor man requires wood he must pay double for it. . . . It is our opinion in regard to a wood, which has fallen into the hands of a lord, whether spiritual or temporal, that unless it was duly purchased it should revert again to the community. . . .

The Sixth Article: Our sixth complaint is in regard to the excessive services demanded of us, which are increased from day to day. We ask that this matter be properly looked into so that we shall not continue to be oppressed in this way, and that some gracious consideration be given us, since our forefathers were required only to serve according to the word of God.

The Seventh Article: Seventh, we will not hereafter allow ourselves to be farther oppressed by our lords, but will let them demand only what is just and proper according to the word of the agreement between the lord and the peasant. . . .

The Eighth Article: In the eighth place, we are greatly burdened by holdings which cannot support the rent exacted from them. The peasants suffer loss in this way and are ruined; and we ask that the lords may appoint persons of honor to inspect these holdings, and fix a rent in accordance with justice, so that the peasant shall not work for nothing, since the laborer is worthy of his hire.

The Ninth Article: In the ninth place, we are burdened with a great evil in the constant making of new laws. We are not judged according to the offence, but sometimes with great ill will, and sometimes much too leniently. In our opinion we should be judged according to the old written law, so that the case shall be decided on its merits, and not with partiality.

The Tenth Article: In the tenth place, we are aggrieved by the appropriation by individuals of meadows and fields which at one time belonged to a community. These we will take again into our own hands . . . .

In these economic demands, the "word of God" was linked with issues of social justice, and the Twelve Articles began and ended with even more dramatic religious demands and claims.

The First Article: First, it is our humble petition and desire, as also our will and resolution, that in the future we should have power and authority so that each community should choose and appoint a pastor, and that we should have the right to depose him should he conduct himself improperly. The pastor thus chosen should teach us the Gospel pure and simple, without any addition, doctrine or ordinance of man. . . .

Conclusion: In the twelfth place it is our conclusion and final resolution, that if one or more of the articles here set forth should not be in agreement with the word of God, as we think they are, such article we will willingly recede from, when it is proved really to be against the word of God by a clear explanation of the scripture.

Although peasant grievances long predated the Reformation, the ideas of Luther and Zwingli about Christian freedom, the importance of Scripture, and the reshaping of Christian life certainly influenced the way peasant calls for change were expressed. Luther immediately responded hostilely, however, in *Against the Robbing and Murdering Hordes of Peasants*, published in 1525. Although peasants and urban rebels sometimes found support for their ideas among radical reformers, Luther and other mainstream reformers asserted that their religious message was not to be linked with economic, social, or political grievances, and that spiritual reasons never gave individuals the right to oppose political authority by force. Peasant armies were crushed with vengeance by the experienced soldiers of the emperor's army, and Luther's words appeared to many to justify the brutality.

They betake themselves to violence, and rob and rage and act like mad dogs. By this it is easy to see what they had in their false minds, and that the pretences which they made in their twelve articles, under the name of the Gospel, were nothing but lies. It is the devil's work that they are at . . .

This cover of a small German pamphlet from 1525 shows an angry crowd of peasants bristling with weapons and farm implements, with a title indicating it contains the "articles and demands of the mob and hoard of peasants who have all banded together." The Twelve Articles of the peasants were published by printers favorable to the peasants, but they were also published, as in this example, by their opponents as a warning of what might happen if such a "mob" was successful.

The peasants have taken on themselves the burden of three terrible sins against God and man, by which they have abundantly merited death in body and soul. In the first place they have sworn to be true and faithful, submissive and obedient, to their rulers, as Christ commands . . . . Because they are breaking this obedience, and are setting themselves against the higher powers, willfully and with violence, they have forfeited body and soul, as faithless, perjured, lying, disobedient knaves and scoundrels are wont to do . . . . In the second place, they are starting a rebellion, and violently robbing and plundering monasteries and castles which are not theirs, by which they have a second time deserved death . . . . Therefore let everyone who can, smite, slay and stab, secretly or openly, remembering that nothing can be more poisonous, hurtful or devilish than a rebel. It is just as when one must kill a mad dog; if you do not strike him, he will strike you, and a whole land with you. In the third place, they cloak this terrible and horrible sin with the Gospel, call themselves "Christian brethren," receive oaths and homage, and compel people to hold with them to these abominations. Thus they become the greatest of all blasphemers of God and slanderers of his holy Name, serving the devil, under the outward appearance of the Gospel, thus earning death in body and soul ten times over.

A Mystic Reformer

The Reformation led some to call for dramatic social change, and led many—both Protestants and Catholics—to engage in public acts in defense of their faith, basing their actions on the words of the Bible or the traditions of the Church. A few individuals, drawing on the long tradition of mysticism in Christianity, understood their ideas to come from direct encounters with God, experienced through seeing visions or hearing voices. One of the most influential mystics of the sixteenth century was Teresa of Ávila, who also became one of the most important Catholic reformers and thinkers of all time. Teresa entered a convent in Spain when she was a teenager, and spent her time in prayer and contemplation. She began to have intense mystical experiences of Christ and the angels, and when she was in her forties, felt a call to turn her visions into action. She founded a convent in her native city of Ávila in which residents followed strict rules of poverty. Teresa's reforming activities set her in opposition to the city leaders of Ávila and many officials in the Spanish church, who thought the life she proposed was too strict for women, particularly those from well-off families. At one point she was even investigated by the Spanish Inquisition, in an effort to make sure her inspiration came

St. Teresa of Ávila has a mystical vision of paradise as an angel pierces her heart, in this seventeenth-century marble statue by the Italian sculptor Gian Lorenzo Bernini. This statue portrays Teresa as if she is in an ecstatic trance, which is how she described experiencing her visions. But she also regarded the visions as a call to reform the Catholic Church in Spain.

from God and not the devil. Pressure from supporters led the process against her to be dropped, and she spent the last years of her life traveling around Spain, establishing new convents and reforming existing ones to bring them back to stricter standards of asceticism and poverty. Some Catholic officials opposed her actions as improper for a woman, but she saw them as a defense of her faith against Protestant challenges. Although she saw herself as an opponent of Protestantism, her language about the power of God and the freedom this brings to those who have faith also provides many similarities with the words of Luther.

One night I was so unwell that I thought I might be excused making my prayer; so I took my rosary, that I might employ myself in vocal prayer . . . I remained there but a few moments thus, when I was rapt in spirit with such violence that I could make no resistance whatever. It seemed to me that I was taken up to heaven; and the first persons I saw there were my father and my mother. I saw other things also . . . . It happened, also, as time went on, and it happens now from time to time, that our Lord showed me still greater secrets. The soul, even if it would, has neither the means nor the power to see more than what He shows it; and so, each time, I saw nothing more than what our Lord was pleased to let me see. But such was the vision, that the least part of it was enough to make my soul amazed, and to raise it so high that it esteems and counts as nothing all the things of this life. I wish I could describe, in some measure, the smallest portion of what I saw; but when I think of doing it, I find it impossible; for the mere difference alone between the light we have here below, and that which is seen in a vision,—both being light,—is so great, that there is no comparison between them . . . . I was in this state once for more than an hour, our Lord showing me wonderful things. He seemed as if He would not leave me. He said to me, "See, My daughter, what they lose who are against Me; do not fail to tell them of it." Ah, my Lord, how little good my words will do them, who are made blind by their own conduct, if Thy Majesty will not give them light! . . . Afterwards I wished I had continued in that trance for ever, and that I had not returned to consciousness, because of an abiding sense of contempt for everything here below; all seemed to be filth; and I see how meanly we employ ourselves who are detained on earth . . . A soul in this state attains to a certain freedom, which is so complete that none can understand it who does not possess it. It is a real and true detachment, independent of our efforts; God effects it all Himself; for His Majesty reveals the truth in such a way, that it remains so deeply impressed on our souls as to make it clear that we of ourselves could not thus acquire it in so short a time . . . . The fear of death, also, was now very slight in me, who had always been in great dread of it; now it seems to me that death is a very light thing for one who serves God, because the soul is in a moment delivered thereby out of its prison, and at rest. This elevation of the spirit, and the vision of things so high, in these trances seem to me to have a great likeness to the flight of the soul from the body, in that it finds itself in a moment in the possession of these good things.

CHAPTER 8

A New Moral Order

This seventeenth-century Dutch painting shows exactly the kind of behavior that Catholic and Protestant moralists sought to combat. A disheveled woman lies passed out from drinking, while a drunken man pours yet another glass from a pitcher. At the rear a servant and two musicians steal the man's coat, while the unmade bed suggests both unrestrained sex and slovenly housekeeping.

Religious reformers, both Protestant and Catholic, and the political authorities who supported them regarded correct belief as crucial. To teach people proper doctrine, they tried to improve clerical education, opened schools for lay people as well as clergy, and encouraged or required attendance at sermons or other services. They also sought to make their states and their communities more moral and orderly. Catholic theologians believed that without good works individuals could not call on God's saving power, whereas Protestant theologians saw pious actions as the fruit of a saving faith given by God. Thus for both Catholics and Protestants, one's sexual, leisure, and workplace activities—and those of one's neighbors—continued to be important in God's eyes. Order, piety, and morality were marks of divine favor. Some leaders initially hoped that simply presenting people with true doctrine would be enough to change their opinions and their behavior, but it quickly became clear that more extensive measures would be needed. Thus beginning in the mid-1500s, almost all religious authorities, whether Protestant or Catholic, supported means of enforcement. In Catholic areas the power of bishops and church courts was strengthened and in Protestant areas special courts were established to handle marriage and morals cases. Officials began to keep registers of marriages, births, baptisms, and deaths, which allowed them better to monitor the people's actions.

This new moral order is often associated with John Calvin, a second-generation reformer who built on the ideas of Luther. Calvin was born and educated as a lawyer in France, but fled to Switzerland when he became a Protestant. There he led the Reformation in the city of

Geneva. He preached, taught, organized new institutions for enforcing discipline and providing public welfare, and set up an academy for young men who wished to become clergy. This school provided them with theological instruction and practical, on-the-job training as local chaplains or assistant pastors before sending them out on their own. Young men trained at the Genevan Academy spread Calvinist ideas into France, the Netherlands, Germany, England, Scotland, Hungary, and Poland, often working with local leaders who had visited or been religious refugees in Geneva and been impressed by what they saw. In areas that were officially Catholic, such as France and the Netherlands, they organized churches secretly. In areas that were Protestant, such as England, they worked within the state church to move theology and discipline in a Calvinist direction, which came to be called Puritanism. In some areas, including Scotland and parts of the Netherlands and Germany, Calvinism became the state church. Religious wars of the second half of the sixteenth century, especially those in France and the Netherlands, primarily involved Calvinist Protestants fighting Catholics. John Calvin's writings were fewer than Luther's, but their global impact was greater.

Marriage was at the center of reformers' moral order. Many ancient and medieval Christian thinkers, most of them monks, had criticized marriage, sometimes in scathing and vicious language; for them, marriage was an inferior sort of Christian life, and their own vows of poverty, chastity, and obedience put them on a better path. Despite these sentiments, however, in the twelfth century the Catholic Church declared that marriage was a sacrament, that is, a ceremony that conferred special grace. Marriage was thus officially indissoluble and divorce was not allowed, although people found various ways to get out of an unwanted marriage. By the fifteenth century, many Catholic writers, particularly Christian humanists, viewed marriage more positively, noting that it was an institution created by God. Marital households were the building blocks of society, they argued, and city leaders agreed, for stable households were the best way to assure moral order. The Protestant reformers were even stronger in their support of marriage. They believed that a priest's or nun's vows of celibacy went against human nature and God's commandments, and that marriage brought spiritual advantages and so was the ideal state for nearly all human beings. Marriage offered husbands and wives companionship and consolation, they asserted, and provided a site for the pious rearing of the next generation of God-fearing Christians.

Convincing people to be God-fearing, teaching them correct belief, and showing them the proper way to behave proved to be difficult. Most studies of the Reformation used to focus primarily on the reformers' *ideas, and they concentrated on the early and middle of the sixteenth century. Now historians focus more on the actual impact of the Protestant and Catholic Reformations, and they examine a much longer sweep of time. They debate the extent to which the reformers' measures were successful, but on one issue there is no dispute: The process lasted well beyond the sixteenth century, because educating people and encouraging (or forcing) them to alter their behavior took far longer than either Protestant or Catholic reformers anticipated.*

Calvin's Geneva

Under the leadership of John Calvin, the Swiss city of Geneva experienced the moral and institutional reforms that accompanied the Reformation with particular intensity. Calvin used his legal training in reasoning to further Protestant ideas to what he saw as their logical outcome. If God is all-powerful and human faith comes from God, Calvin reasoned, then there is no free will. As he explained in the *Institutes of the Christian Religion*, a long theological treatise first published in 1536 and expanded many times after that, all humans are sinful and on their own merits would go to hell, but instead God decided that some would be saved, an idea Calvin called "predestination" or "election."

By predestination we mean the eternal decree of God, by which he determined with himself whatever he wished to happen with regard to every man. All are not created on equal terms, but some are preordained to eternal life, others to eternal damnation; and, accordingly, as each has been created for one or other of these ends, we say that he has been predestined to life or to death . . . .

We say, then, that Scripture clearly proves this much, that God by his eternal and immutable counsel determined once for all those whom it was his pleasure one day to admit to salvation, and those whom, on the other hand, it was his pleasure to doom to destruction. We maintain that this counsel, as regards the elect [that is, those chosen for salvation], is founded on his free mercy, without any respect to human worth, while those whom he dooms to destruction are excluded from access to life by a just and blameless, but at the same time incomprehensible judgment.

An engraving from 1574 shows an older Calvin dressed in the clothes of a scholar and teacher. The German rhyme underneath by an anonymous supporter of Calvin notes that just as Luther taught the Germans, so Calvin has increased belief among the French, and defeated the devil and the anti-Christ.

Although you might think that this would be a very depressing idea and would lead people to just do whatever they wanted, it actually had the opposite effect. Calvinists came to believe that hard work, thrift, and proper moral conduct were signs that you were among the "elect" chosen for salvation. Business or personal success was taken as a further sign of salvation. Merchants and craftsmen in prosperous cities were attracted to Calvinism because of the sense of purpose it offered. Calvin put his ideas into action in Geneva, encouraging city leaders to issue ordinances in 1547 that regulated many aspects of life.

In this 1514 engraving by Albrecht Dürer, a peasant couple dances at village festivities of some sort. Dancing was one of the activities that Calvinists in Geneva and elsewhere attempted to prohibit or control, viewing it as a waste of time and an encouragement to immoral behavior. Laws prohibiting dancing were regularly broken, however, as everyone from peasants to kings danced.

Blasphemy

Whoever shall have blasphemed, swearing by the body or by the blood of our Lord, or in similar manner, he shall be made to kiss the earth for the first offence; for the second to pay 5 sous, and for the third 6 sous, and for the last offence be put in the pillory for one hour.

Drunkenness

1. That no one shall invite another to drink under penalty of 3 sous.
2. That taverns shall be closed during the sermon, under penalty that the tavern-keeper shall pay 3 sous, and whoever may be found therein shall pay the same amount.
3. If any one be found intoxicated he shall pay for the first offence 3 sous and shall be remanded to the consistory; for the second offence he shall be held to pay the same sum of 6 sous, and for the third 10 sous and be put in prison.

Songs and Dances

If any one sing immoral, dissolute or outrageous songs, or dance the virollet or other dance, he shall be put in prison for three days and then sent to the consistory.

Games

That no one shall play at any dissolute game or at any game whatsoever it may be, neither for gold nor silver nor for any excessive stake, upon penalty of 5 sous and forfeiture of the stake played for.

As noted in the laws, the punishments stipulated for breaking them included fines, public shaming, and being called before the consistory. The consistory kept thorough records of the Genevans called before it, as in this 1542 case of a cobbler who engaged in conduct judged improper.

Thursday August 24, 1542

Jaques Bornant, called Callaz, cobbler [Summoned] because of [absence from] the sermons and wasting time in gambling games. Answers that he goes to the sermons on Sundays. Said the [Lord's] prayer and the confession [Creed] and does not know the commandments. The consistory advises that he be admonished to cease to gamble to give an example to others, and to frequent the sermons.

Pillory
A wooden frame set up in a public place, in which a person's head and hands could be locked

Consistory
A group of pastors and lay men charged with investigating and disciplining people accused of improper doctrine or conduct

Discipline is the sinews of the church.
—Motto of the Calvinist consistory in Nimes, France, established in 1561

Marriage and the Reformation

Law courts and consistories were important institutions in the battle for moral order, but for Calvin, and for every other Protestant reformer as well, the most important institution in this effort was the marital household. Protestants rejected the value of celibacy, and stressed that marriage had been ordained by God when he presented Eve to Adam. In a sermon preached in January 1525, Luther described marriage in metaphors that his hearers would easily understand. Six months later, Luther put his words into practice, and married Katharina von Bora, a former nun; the marriage produced six children.

God has laid a serious command upon marriage. Just like a gardener who, having a lovely herb or rose garden that he loves and does not want anyone to climb in and break anything off or do damage to it, builds a fence around it. God does just this with the Sixth Commandment: "You shall not commit adultery." For marriage is His [God's] most beloved herb or rose garden, in which the most beautiful roses and carnations grow, and these are the dear children of humans, who are created in the image of God. They come out and are born so that the human race is maintained. So God bids one to keep marriage in the fear of God, in modesty and honor, and not to

This double portrait of a well-to-do Dutch couple from about 1540 was most likely painted for their wedding. Such wedding portraits graced the walls and shelves of middle- and upper-class homes, and were even worn as lockets, testifying to the importance of marriage.

A family portrait of an English nobleman from the early seventeenth century shows him surrounded by his wife and children, with the family estate stretching out beyond the curtain at the back. Such family portraits depicted both hierarchy and intimacy. The wife looks at her husband, although he does not look at her, and her head is lower than his, but he is also touching her arm and has his arm around one of his sons.

commit adultery. For whoever commits adultery God will punish horribly in body and soul and cast out of His kingdom.

Most other Protestant reformers also married, and their wives had to create a new and respectable role for themselves—pastor's wife. They were living demonstrations of their husband's convictions about the superiority of marriage to celibacy, and were expected to be models of pious living and Christian charity. Pastors' wives were also expected to be models of wifely obedience, for Protestants did not break with medieval theologians in their idea that women were subject to men, as Luther states plainly in his 1525 sermon on marriage, again using metaphors drawn from everyday life.

"Women, be subject to your husbands as to the Lord, for the husband is the head of the wife" [Eph. 5:22-23]. Because of this, the wife has not been created out of the head, so that she shall not rule over her husband, but be subject and obedient to him.

For that reason the wife wears a headdress, that is, the veil on her head, as St. Paul writes in I Corinthians in the second chapter, that she is not free but under obedience to her husband.

The wife veils herself with a fine, soft veil, spun and sewn out of pretty, soft flax or linen; and she does not wind a coarse bunch of woven fabric or a dirty cloth around her head or mouth. Why does she do this? So that she speaks fine, lovely, friendly words to her husband and not coarse, filthy, scolding words, as the bad wives who carry a sword in their mouths.

Truth it is, that women must specially feel the griefs and pains of matrimony, in that they relinquish the liberty of their own rule, in the pain of their labor and delivery, in the bringing up of their own children, in which offices they be in great perils, and be grieved with many afflictions, which they might be without, if they lived out of matrimony.

—1567 homily on marriage, which English monarchs required to be read out loud regularly in all English churches

Divorce

Catholic doctrine forbade divorce, whereas most Protestants came to allow it, usually for adultery, impotence, desertion, conviction for a capital crime, or deadly assault. This dramatic change in marital law had a less than dramatic impact, however. Because marriage was the cornerstone of society socially and economically, divorce was a desperate last resort, and Protestant authorities granted divorces only in extreme cases. In many Protestant jurisdictions, the annual divorce rate hovered around 0.02 to 0.06 per thousand people. (By contrast, the 2000 U.S. divorce rate was 4.1 per thousand people.) In addition, Catholicism did allow annulment and "separation from bed and board," so couples who could not stand to stay with one another could sometimes find a way out of the marriage, although separated couples could not remarry. Catholic authorities were also more willing than Protestants to allow abused wives to live separately from their husbands.

Luther also had words in this sermon for husbands.

Men should govern their wives not with great cudgels, flails, or drawn knives, but rather with friendly words and gestures and with all gentleness so that they do not become shy . . . and take fright such that they afterward do not know what to do. Thus, men should rule their wives with reason and not unreason, and honor the feminine sex as the weakest vessel and also as co-heirs of the grace of life.

To Protestants, a respectable marriage reflected both the spiritual equality of men and women and the proper social hierarchy of husbandly authority and wifely obedience. Catholic reformers agreed. As with so many other issues, Catholic thinkers reaffirmed traditional doctrine in response to Protestants and continued to assert that the most worthy type of Christian life was one both celibate and chaste. They also presented more positive views of marriage than had medieval Catholic thinkers, however. In a sermon on marriage preached in Munich in the early seventeenth century, the popular Catholic preacher Geminianus Monacensis used a painting of a cherub surrounded by lilies and palm trees to symbolize the social order established by God. The cherub stood for the celibate priesthood, the lilies were virginal nuns and chaste widows, and the palm trees were married folk.

Enlightened by God, Solomon wanted to prefigure with his temple's adornments in what way the Holy Christian Catholic Church was going to be adorned with three kinds of estates: the first being the ecclesiastical epitomized through the Angel Cherub. . . . The lilies [next] are an image of the virginal [estate] and the chaste estate of the widow. . . . The third adornment of God's church is the holy estate of matrimony represented by the palm trees; it appears as if God created this plant for this very end as to be a mirror for the spouses . . . these plants have such love for one another they cannot bear fruit without each other . . . as soon as they get close to one another . . . their roots . . . intertwine to such a degree that no human being can dissolve them . . . . In between these images of marriage Solomon places the Cherub in order to explain: Who is it that must unite these two loving plants? The Angel, that is the Priest: after this kind of union has taken place the two plants can never be divorced again.

Preaching and Teaching

To both Protestant and Catholic leaders, sermons seemed the perfect place to teach people what they were supposed to believe and how they were to act. In 1545, Pope Paul III called together an ecumenical council of church officials to define Catholic doctrine and reform abuses. The council, which met in Trent in northern Italy off and on over an eighteen-year period, issued many decrees stipulating reforms and reasserting traditional Catholic beliefs in response to both humanists and Protestants. Among these were decrees stipulating the content of sermons.

In order that the faithful people may approach to the reception of the sacraments with greater reverence and devotion of mind, the holy Council commands all bishops, that, not only when they are themselves about to administer them to the people, they shall first explain, in a manner suited to the capacity of those who receive them, the efficacy and use of those sacraments, but shall endeavour that the same be done piously and prudently by every parish priest; and this even in the vernacular tongue, if need be . . . as also that, during the solemnization of mass, or the celebration of the divine offices, they explain, in the said vulgar tongue, on all festivals or solemnities, the divine commands, and the maxims of salvation; and that, setting aside all unprofitable questions, they endeavour to impress these things on the hearts of all, and to instruct them in the law of the Lord.

German Protestant leaders similarly issued ordinances about the content of sermons, which were not only to explain doctrine but also instruct people in a wide range of Christian duties, as described in this ordinance from the duchy of Württemberg in 1559.

At least twice a year, once in spring and again on the approach of winter, each pastor shall make in his sermons serious admonition to his parishioners that they must be diligent in sending their children to school. And let him stress the great benefit bound to come from this, schools being necessary not only for learning the liberal arts, but also the fear of God, virtue, and discipline. Where the young are neglected and kept out of school, permanent harm, both eternal and temporal, must result, as children grow up without fear and knowledge of God, without discipline, like the dumb beasts

L'ASSEMBLEE DU CONCILE DE TRENTE.

1. L'Orateur du Roy Philippe.
2. Le Secretaire du Concile.
3. Le Theologien raportant son opinion.
4. Les Cardinaux.
5. Les Legats du Siege Apostol.
6. Les Orateurs Ecclesiastiques.
7. Les Orateurs Laics.
8. Les deux Courriers.

In this French illustration of the opening session of the Council of Trent, churchmen sit in orderly rows, listening to a speaker. The Council of Trent reaffirmed traditional Catholic doctrine on all points, although it also called for the reform of abuses and better education for priests so that they could explain these doctrines in ways their parishioners would understand.

This is the title page of Luther's 1529 small catechism, which contained explanations of the Ten Commandments, the Lord's Prayer, and other basic documents of Christian faith, designed to help pastors and parents teach young people. The catechism is still used in instruction in Lutheran churches around the world today.

of the field, learning nothing about what is needed for their salvation, nor what is useful to them and their neighbors in worldly life. And the pastor shall inform them, furthermore, that school-mastering is a troublesome office and laborious, thankless work for which teachers should be honored and respected, and their hard-earned pay given to them willingly and without grudge.

Teaching children was not to be limited to school hours, however, as the Protestant pastor and schoolmaster Christoph Vischer noted in his explanation of the catechism (a basic statement of beliefs), a book written for parents and published in 1573.

In addition [to public instruction and examinations] all parents are obliged on danger of losing their souls to teach the catechism to their children and domestic servants. Every day, let your children recite

the main articles of the catechism, taking care that they speak clearly and pronounce distinctly. Ask them also what they remember from last Sunday's sermon, and, if they remember nothing, admonish them to pay closer attention. And if kind words don't help, take the stick to them or give them nothing to eat and drink for supper until they have repeated something from the sermon.

This somewhat idealized view of a city school in Calvin's Geneva reflects the aims of the Protestant reformers, who advocated the founding of schools to teach children reading skills, religious doctrine, and proper behavior. Funding for these schools was often difficult to arrange, and many fewer were opened than reformers had hoped.

Were the Reformers Successful?

It is easy to find *prescriptive* evidence such as sermons, ordinances, and law codes that set out the goals and measures of secular and religious authorities as they tried to shape a pious and moral society. *Descriptive* evidence comes from the institutions established to carry out these aims, such as schools, law courts, and investigative bodies. Among these were visitations—inspection tours by religious authorities in which they travelled from village to village. A Catholic visitation team in Spain in 1566 found that rules about taverns were widely disregarded.

His majesty is informed that on past visits Gregario Gomez and Alonso Galente, inhabitants of Dacon, Jaun de Momdian and Jaun Bernáldez, inhabitants of Toscana, and Gabriel de Dacon, all tavern owners, were

This tavern sign from seventeenth-century London conveys the name of the tavern—the Ape and Apple—to those who could not read, so that all who passed knew clearly what could be purchased within. Despite the best efforts of Protestant and Catholic authorities, taverns throughout Europe continued to offer a different sort of break from daily work and woes than that offered by sermons and psalm-singing.

admonished not to open the taverns nor sell wine, bread or meat to the parishioners on Sundays and holidays before High Mass. They have not wanted to comply, opening the taverns and selling wine and meat so that the parishioners quit coming to Mass in order to be there playing and drinking. Being compassionate with them he has fined each one of them three reales [a small coin] for the fabric of the church for this first time, except Alonso Galente who is fined only one and a half reales on account of his poverty. Henceforth, they will be fined one ducat [a much larger gold coin] for each time that they open them during Mass.

A Lutheran visitation report from central Germany in 1594—seventy years after the introduction of the Protestant Reformation in this area— found even more problems.

First, gruesome cursing and blaspheming, as for instance "by God," "by God's Holy Cross," "by God's Passion, -death, -flesh, -blood, -heart, -hand," etc., "A Thousand Sacraments," "by the Baptism," "element," "star," "thunder and hail," "earth." Also dreadful swearing by various fears, epidemics, and injuries. These oaths are very common among young and old, women as well as men. People cannot carry on a friendly chat, or even address their children, without the use of these words. And none of them considers it a sin to swear.

Everyone is lax about going to church, both young and old. Many have not been seen by their pastor in a year or more .... Those who come to service are usually drunk. As soon as they sit down they lean their head on their arms and sleep through the whole sermon, except that sometimes they fall off the benches, making a great clatter, or women drop their babies on the floor .... At times the wailing of babies is so loud that the preacher cannot make himself heard in the church.

The moment the sermon ends, everyone runs out. No one stays for the hymn, prayer, and blessing. They behave as if they were at a dance, not a divine service ....

Visitation reports always present a dismal—although colorful—picture. The records from other types of institutions suggest that on at least a few issues, the goals of the reformers were being achieved to some degree. In Catholic areas, the Inquisition had jurisdiction over cases involving incorrect belief and moral lapses, and beginning in the late sixteenth century it found gradual improvements in people's abilities to recite the Lord's Prayer, the Ten Commandments, and other prayers. The Calvinist

consistory in Geneva also found a few signs that the Protestant message was getting across.

Thursday, February 8, 1543
Master Guy the shearer . . . answers that he wants to live and die according to the Reformation . . . He cannot go to the sermons because of his affairs, but goes to the catechism, and is not a papist, and was at the sermon last Sunday.

Sometimes, in fact, ordinary people went beyond what reformers had anticipated. They not only listened to what their pastors and priests taught them, but then held religious officials themselves to the same standards. Parishioners in the small German Catholic village of Rülzheim, for example, complained in a letter to the bishop about their local priest.

We pray to God that we could get rid of their quarrelsome and troublesome priest. We want to behave as good Catholic Christians should, but all we get from him is abuse, ridicule, and insults.

Bishops had the power to appoint priests in Catholic parts of Europe, but in some Protestant areas parishioners themselves played a role in selecting their pastors. Church and government officials hoped that villagers would obediently agree to whoever they chose, but this was not always the case. Religious change in this era did not always come from the top down, but was sometimes a process of negotiation between ordinary people and their superiors. In a 1606 petition to a church superintendent, the villagers of Ebsdorf parish in central Germany asserted their independence, and indicated that they would be the ones to decide who would be instructing them about how they should live and what God wanted.

We respectfully affirm the following: One of our neighbors, Balthasar Fischer, sent his son, whose name is Heinrich Fischer, to

People gathered for a church festival engage in all sorts of activities: They get married, have their teeth pulled, dance, gamble, buy merchandise from stalls, drink wine and beer, and suffer from the effects of too much drinking. Protestant authorities sometimes banned church festivals because they thought they encouraged sinful behavior, but such bans were not always effective, and people held festivals anyway.

study at great expense. By God's grace he continued until he had learned all the duties of the pastoral office well, and was given a position as the regular pastor in the congregation of Altenhassell in the duchy of Hanau. We then fervently asked that he would be given to us as a pastor because he was the son of one of our neighbors . . . But because of his duties there, the above-mentioned Heinrich Fischer could not be freed from his position, so we asked your honor if there was another person who would be suitable. We came to an agreement, which your honor approved, that the pastor of Walgern should give a sermon at our church, so that we could see if we approved of him. Not only was this to happen, but the village mayor was to order every citizen in each village of this parish, man for man, to attend this service and listen to the sermon. At the end of the service, the mayor was to speak with each man individually to get a clear idea of whether each of them was happy with this pastor or not. This then happened as it was supposed to. Not only did everyone individually say yes, but the whole parish did communally as well. In addition, the parish said that they were also satisfied with the other actions that their elected representatives had already taken in regards to this matter,

An altar painting from a Danish church shows religious practice as Protestant reformers hoped it would be, with pious believers listening to sermons, bringing their children to be baptized, and taking communion in the Protestant way, that is, with the clergy giving lay believers both the bread and the wine. Actual religious practice did not always live up to this ideal, but by the end of the sixteenth century in both Catholic and Protestant areas people did have a slightly better idea of Christian doctrine than they had had at the beginning of the century.

Masked women in elaborate dress mix with actors and musicians wearing costumes in this later sixteenth-century engraving of the carnival before Lent in Venice. Protestants objected to carnival because they saw it as a Catholic practice, and also because wearing masks allowed people to hide their identity and mingle in ways that upset the social order.

as well as actions that they would take in the future for the good of this poor parish. So we ask, both as a group and individually, that you appoint this pastor as a teacher and pastoral shepherd. Hopefully, it will honor God, be of good to you, and yield the most good to us poor people.

SVLIMAN · OTOMAN · REX · TVRCX

Die Cron dieses Tuckischen Keysers Solimani
ist geschätzt auf fünffmal hundert tausend ducaten.

der Asmaral
80000 ungar

CHAPTER 9

Global Connections and Challenges

The Renaissance and the Reformation happened in one small corner of the world, but they soon came to have global effects. At the same time that Michelangelo was carving magnificent statues and Martin Luther was publishing works attacking the Catholic Church, European sailors, merchants, and explorers were venturing over new sea routes. Their voyages took them around the coast of Africa into the Indian Ocean, and then across the Atlantic to what they at first dubbed "the Indies" (thinking they were near China and India) and then the "New World." Overseas explorations and the colonies founded as a result of these journeys eventually transformed Europe into the dominant power in the world. That story takes us far beyond Europe itself, and far beyond the Renaissance and Reformation, but an examination of some aspects of European exploration gives a broader perspective on the economic changes, social transformations, and intellectual developments of this era.

Many different factors motivated European voyages. Early explorers and those who supported them often hoped to counter Muslim power, or at least to find ways around Muslim merchants and trade directly with distant lands. Christian authorities saw newly conquered lands as places to win converts and expand the faith. Kings and queens increasingly regarded lands beyond Europe as sources of needed raw materials and important symbols of their power. The primary driving force in exploration and colonization, however, was the desire for wealth.

In this era, great riches came primarily through trade. In the late fourteenth century, despite the Commercial Revolution and the expansion of business in Europe, the most important trading network in the

In the early sixteenth century, Venetian goldsmiths made an enormous helmet encrusted with pearls and jewels specifically for Sultan Suleiman the Magnificent, the ruler of the Ottoman Empire. They made it larger than the crowns worn by the pope or emperor, and sold it to Suleiman for an enormous sum. He most likely never wore it, but displayed it as a sign of his wealth and power. European overseas voyages were, in part, an attempt to counter that power and establish trade connections that were not in Muslim hands.

world was the Indian Ocean. Indian, Arab, Malay, Persian, and Turkish merchants, many of them Muslim, controlled the trade in spices and other luxuries in Asia and the Near East. Once goods got to Cairo or Constantinople they were often handled by European merchants, most of whom were Christian. These merchants came especially from northern Italian cities such as Venice, Genoa, Pisa, and Florence.

Many merchants and political leaders in other parts of Europe resented the Muslim and Italian dominance of trade, and sought ways to counteract it. Among these was Prince Henry of Portugal, who sponsored ships sailing down the coast of Africa looking for gold and opportunities to trade. Henry eventually planned and raised the money for more than fifty voyages, and also supported mapmakers, astronomers, and mathematicians, who made charts and calculations to assist the ships' captains, for which he was later dubbed "the Navigator."

Portuguese ships inched down the African coast, and discovered islands in the Atlantic, where Henry encouraged colonization and farming, especially raising sugar cane. In the 1450s a Genoese merchant under Henry's sponsorship made direct contact with the Mali Empire of West Africa. With this the amount of trade increased dramatically. Europeans traded guns, cloth, and other manufactured goods for African gold and slaves. A few of these West African slaves, captured in raids or sold into slavery further in the interior, went to Europe, but most went initially to the sugar plantations of the new Portuguese colonies on the Atlantic islands.

Portuguese voyages down the west coast of Africa offered the promise of wealth for ambitious young men, who flocked to Lisbon from many parts of Europe. One of these was Christopher Columbus, who had grown up in the bustling Italian port city of Genoa. Columbus joined the crew of a merchant ship when he was a teenager, then settled in Lisbon and married a woman whose father was one of Henry the Navigator's captains and a governor of one of the Portuguese Atlantic islands, where the couple lived for some time. From his reading of classical geographers and medieval travelers, and his conversations with sailors and mapmakers, Columbus developed a new plan for obtaining Asian silks and spices—sail westward rather than around Africa. Columbus took his plan to the Portuguese court, where the king's council firmly rejected it, because they knew Columbus's estimations of the distance from Europe to Asia going westward were far too short, and a voyage taking this route would be too costly.

Columbus next tried the Spanish court, where for many years he got the same reaction, but in 1492 the Spanish monarchs Isabella and Ferdinand changed their minds and agreed to support him. Traveling with three small ships, Columbus carried Chinese silk in his sea chests, figuring that wherever he landed, people would know about this beautiful fabric and could direct him to where it was made. He also brought along an Arabic-speaking Spaniard as a translator, figuring that with all the trade around the Indian Ocean and South China Sea, someone at the Chinese court certainly spoke Arabic.

Columbus, as we all know, never found China, but his first voyage to the islands that he called the "Indies" electrified Europe, with his reports of amazing natural products, the possibility of gold, and new sorts of people. He had eager volunteers for his second voyage, which involved seventeen ships, crowded with more than a thousand men. These included priests who wished to convert the indigenous peoples to Christianity and colonists intending to settle on the islands, but mostly men looking for easy riches. They were sadly disappointed, and many went home again after only a few weeks, for there was no gold or other riches to be found. Hoping to gain wealth through agriculture, the Spanish began to experiment with different types of crops, forcing the island peoples to work for them. Many died of disease and harsh treatment—a pattern repeated throughout the Americas—and the Spanish decided that the only way to solve their need for labor was to import slaves from Africa. First thousands and then tens of thousands of people were taken from Africa every year to work on agricultural plantations in the Americas. European conquest and colonization thus dramatically altered the history of Africa, as well as that of the New World.

Slavery was a part of many societies around the world in 1500, but the plantation slavery of the Americas was different from earlier slavery in two ways. One of these was the fact that almost all the slaves were black, and almost all the owners and managers were white. Plantation slavery had a racial element that slavery in other parts of the world did not. The second new thing about plantation slavery was how much it depended on the new international trading networks created as a result of European voyages. Plantations only grew one thing, which meant that everything else needed on the plantation had to be brought in—food, clothing, and tools. We often think of slavery as a very backward system, not modern like factories, but in many ways plantations were factories, mass producing one specific thing to be sold as widely as possible.

The relative ease with which the Spanish conquered large areas of the Americas created a strong sense that Europeans were destined to impose Christianity and civilization on the "new" peoples they encountered. This notion combined with assessments of African inferiority bolstered by the expansion of the African slave trade to create a greater sense of European cultural superiority than had been evident earlier. After the Reformation, Protestant powers such as England and the

Apothecaries' Ingredients

Most illness was handled by home remedies, but city people also relied on apothecaries to prescribe and prepare treatments if they were feeling ill. Many of these were purgatives that induced vomiting in the hope that this would rid the body of whatever was making it ill. The bark of the cassia tree and the root of the scammony plant were imported from Asia and made into purgatives, as were European-grown colocynth fruits and agaric mushrooms. Apothecaries also prescribed medications as antidotes to poison that contained fanciful ingredients such as mithridate or dragon's blood; what these were exactly was a secret the apothecaries did not share with their customers. The voyages to the Americas yielded a range of new plants, minerals, and other natural products that became part of apothecaries' mixtures.

Levant

The eastern Mediterranean, today's Lebanon, Israel, and Syria

Camlet, grogram and samite

Luxury fabrics made of silk and other expensive fibers

Netherlands also established colonies, which provided resources for the battles against Catholics. Whether Catholic or Protestant, European countries gained new territories and sources of wealth from their overseas conquests, and also new confidence in their technical and spiritual supremacy. Through colonization, Renaissance art, including portraits of powerful people done in oil following rules of perspective and marble statuary designed for magnificent churches, and Reformation theology, including the writings of Luther and Loyola, were carried around the world.

The Wealth of the Indies and the Portuguese Voyages

Ships crossed the Indian Ocean carrying silk, cloth, pearls, furs, silver, porcelain dishes, carpets, gems, gold, and spices. Italian merchants, especially Venetians, brought these luxury goods to the rest of Europe, as the Florentine diplomat and historian Francesco Guiccardini reported in 1560 in his description of the Flemish city of Antwerp.

The Venetians dispose in these parts of spices such as clove, cinnamon, nutmeg, ginger, and numerous drugs such as rhubarb, cassia, agaric, dragon's blood, mummy, senna-leaf, colocynth, scammony, tutty, mithridate, and treacle. They draw almost all of these spices and drugs from the Levant ... From Venice likewise are brought here much very beautiful and rich silk cloth, spun and raw silk, camlets, grograms and mohairs, carpets, samites marvellously well made; of excellent scarlets, cottons, cumin, and other small wares of silk and other material. In addition they send indigo and other colours suitable for dyeing and painting.

The wealth brought by trade was a lure attracting enterprising merchants and rulers. Among these was the younger son of the king in a tiny country on the far western end of the Mediterranean, Prince Henry of Portugal. Henry conquered the Muslim city of Ceuta in Morocco in 1415 and became its governor, and then decided to sponsor ships going further south. In this he was motivated by a variety of factors, as the Portuguese historian Gomes Eannes de Azurara reported in *The Chronicle of Guinea*, written in 1453. Azurara emphasizes Henry's opposition to the Muslims, and also mentions his desire to gain wealth and spread Christianity, a common mix of motivations.

After the taking of Ceuta he always kept ships well armed against the Infidel [that is, the Muslims], both for war, and because he had also a wish to know the land that lay beyond the isles of Canary ... and seeing also that no other prince took any pains in this matter, he sent out his own ships against those parts, to have manifest certainty of them all. . . .

The second reason was that if there chanced to be in those lands some population of Christians, or some havens, into which it would be possible to sail without peril, many kinds of merchandise might be brought to this realm, which would find a ready market, and reasonably so, because no other people of these parts traded with them, nor yet people of any other that were known; and also the products of this realm might be taken there, which traffic would bring great profit to our countrymen.

A manuscript from the mid-sixteenth century shows a fleet of Portuguese ships on its way to India in 1519. Portuguese ship builders and captains made use of various combinations of sails to achieve greater speed and maneuverability.

The third reason was that, as it was said that the power of the Moors [Muslims] in that land of Africa was very much greater than was commonly supposed ... and because every wise man is obliged by natural prudence to wish for a knowledge of the power of his enemy. ...

The fourth reason was because during the one and thirty years that he had warred against the Moors, he had never found a Christian king, nor a lord outside this land, who for the love of our Lord Jesus Christ would aid him in the said war. Therefore he sought to know if there were in those parts any Christian princes, in whom the charity and the love of Christ was so ingrained that they would aid him against those enemies of the faith.

The fifth reason was his great desire to make increase in the faith of our Lord Jesus Christ and to bring to him all the souls that should be saved ... by which his spirit may be glorified after this life in the celestial realm.

Portuguese ships first landed on the islands off the west coast of Africa, where the Portuguese established colonies, and then made contact with the people of West Africa, trading for gold and slaves. Portuguese captains continued to press southward in search of more African riches, and in 1497, a small fleet under the command of Vasco da Gama, an experienced sea captain, rounded Africa, and reached Calicut on the west coast of India by sailing directly across the Arabian Sea under the guidance of an African pilot. Indian forces fought da Gama, and he left for Portugal with fewer spices than he had hoped. King Manuel I still rewarded him richly and gave him the title "Admiral of the Indian Ocean." He sent da Gama back three years later, this time with twenty warships. Gaspar Correa, a Portuguese chronicler who traveled to India, described the violent tactics da Gama used in his conquest of Calicut in his history of the Portuguese explorations written in 1515. Correa does not explicitly indicate that he disapproved of these tactics, but the extent to which he includes every gruesome detail suggests that he might have thought da Gama's actions were extreme.

He then ordered all the fleet to draw in close to the shore, and all day, till night, he bombarded the city, by which he made a great destruction; and he did not choose to fire more,

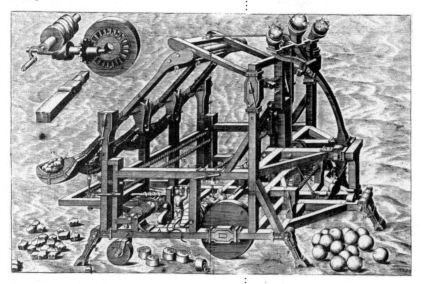

In this sixteenth-century engraving, a machine for flinging rocks and gunpowder-filled cannonballs dwarfs the two men who man it, conveying the artist's sense of the increasing importance of mechanized warfare. Although no machines were actually this size, cannon and artillery were essential to European conquests throughout the world.

on account of the damage received thereby by the ships which had to return to the kingdom . . . [then in six ships] he put as many as two hundred men, amongst whom were many cross-bow men, —for at that time there were not yet any fire-locks,—and he gave them more artillery and munitions. Whilst they were doing this business, there came in two large ships, and twenty-two sambuks and Malabar vessels, laden with rice. . . . He then ordered the boats to go and plunder the small vessels, which were sixteen, and the two ships, in which they found rice, and many jars of butter, and many bales of stuffs. They then gathered all this together into the ships, with the crews of the two large ships, and he ordered all the boats to get as much rice as they wanted, and they took that of four of the small vessels, which they emptied, for they did not want. Then the captain-major commanded them to cut off the hands and ears and noses of all the crews, and put all that into one of the small vessels. . . . When all the Indians had been thus executed, he ordered their feet to be tied together, as they had no hands with which to untie them: and in order that they should not untie them with their teeth, he ordered them to strike upon their teeth with staves, and they knocked them down their throats; and they were thus put on board, heaped up upon the top of each other, mixed up with the blood which streamed from them; and he ordered mats and dry leaves to be spread over them, and the sails to be set for the shore, and the vessel set on fire: and there were more than eight hundred Moors; and the small vessel, with all the hands and ears, was also sent on shore under sail, without being fired. These vessels went at once on shore, where many people flocked together to put out the fire, and draw out those whom they found alive, upon which they made great lamentations.

Da Gama returned to Portugal with a huge amount of spices, gold, jewels, and other plunder, and the king made him a count. In the Indian Ocean, Portuguese mariners built fortified trading posts and required all merchant ships that sailed near to buy licenses or risk having their cargoes confiscated and their captains executed if they met a Portuguese warship. Cannons and sturdy ships made this Portuguese protection racket possible. The Portuguese were far from home, with no backup if they lost, so they were ruthless or even foolhardy against what were always larger local forces. They never came to dominate the centuries-old trade in gold, spices, silk, and other goods the way that they hoped to, but Portuguese ships regularly carried spices to Europe. As Guiccardini reported from Antwerp in 1560, their voyages upset older trading routes through which spices had been carried north from Venice.

sambuk

Small boat with one or two sails, used in the Red Sea, the Gulf of Arabia, and along the Malabar coast, the southwest coast of India

A merchant offers his goods to a wealthy customer in this sixteenth-century German woodcut. The rhyme beneath the picture details all the things he sells, including spices, linen, silk, and wax, but also notes that worry, care, and bad luck often accompany him.

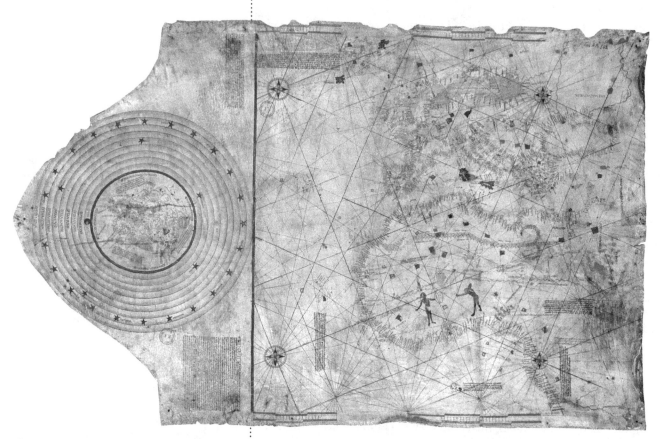

This map made in Lisbon in 1490 shows the extent of Portuguese voyages down the African coast at that point, with very accurate understanding of the coastline. It was made in the mapmaker's workshop of Christopher Columbus and his brother Bartolomeo, who were in Portugal in 1490 attempting to get financial backing for their sail westward. The Portuguese king would not support Columbus because he knew that Columbus's calculations about the size of the earth were wrong, and that continuing to sail down around Africa offered the better possibility of reaching India and China.

The second of the notable advantages which have made the city of Antwerp so great, rich, and famous, began about the year 1503–1504, when the Portuguese, by marvelous and amazing navigation, and with warlike equipment, having, just before, occupied Calicut, made a treaty with the king of that region. They began to transport spices and drugs from India to Portugal and then to carry them from Portugal to the fairs in this city. These spices and drugs were formerly brought by way of the Red Sea to Beirut and Alexandria, and from these places carried by the Venetians to Venice to supply Italy, France, Germany, and other Christian provinces. But once this commerce had been intercepted by the Portuguese, and they had sent an agent to Antwerp in the name of their king, little by little this trade attracted the Germans . . . Not yet knowing anything about the new voyage of the Portuguese, the Germans were so astounded that they doubted the quality of the said spices, and suspected that they were adulterated. This was because the Germans had been accustomed to furnish the people of these lands with the same drugs which came overland from Venice.

The Voyages of Columbus

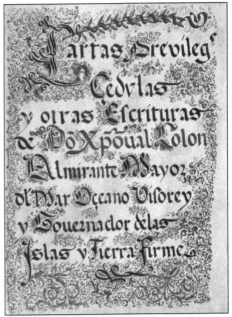

As Portuguese ships sailed further and further down the African coast (but before da Gama rounded the Cape), Christopher Columbus attempted to gain Portuguese sponsorship to try to reach China and India by sailing westward. He was unsuccessful, and was also initially unsuccessful at the Spanish court. The Spanish monarchs, Isabella and Ferdinand, were intensely religious, however, and grew more interested once Columbus told them he planned to use the wealth gained from his trip to recapture Jerusalem from the Muslims. He told them he was destined by God to spread Christianity, a destiny symbolized by his first name, Christo-fero, which means "Christ carrier" in Latin. (Columbus often signed his first name using the Greek symbols for Christ.) In 1492 the monarchs changed their minds, as Columbus himself reported in the logbook of his first voyage. Unsurprisingly, he emphasizes religious aims above all else, and links their decision to support him with their conquest of the last remaining Muslim territory in Spain and their expulsion of the Jews from Spanish lands. This logbook survives only in a copy made later by Bartolomé de las Casas, a friend of the Columbus family who later became a missionary in the Spanish New World colonies.

When Christopher Columbus returned home from his first voyage, Ferdinand and Isabella gave him a series of titles to the lands he had claimed and a coat of arms.

On 2 January in the year 1492, when your Highnesses had concluded their war with the Moors who reigned in Europe, I saw your Highnesses' banners victoriously raised on the towers of the Alhambra, the citadel of that city, and the Moorish king come out of the city gates and kiss the hands of your Highnesses and the prince, My Lord. And later in that same month, on the grounds of information I had given your royal Highnesses concerning the lands of India and a prince who is called the Great Khan—which means in Spanish 'King of Kings'—and of his and his ancestors' frequent and vain application to Rome for men learned in the holy faith who should instruct them in it, your Highnesses decided to send me, Christopher Columbus, to see these parts of India and the princes and people of those lands and consider the best means for their conversion. For, by the neglect of the Popes to send instructors, many nations had fallen to idolatry and adopted doctrines of perdition, and your Highnesses as Catholic princes and devoted propagators of the holy Christian faith have always been enemies of the sect of Mahomet [Muhammad] and of all idolatries and heresies.

Your Highnesses ordained that I should not go eastward by land in the usual manner but by the western way which no one about whom we have positive information has ever followed. Therefore having expelled all the Jews from your dominions in that same

The Legacy of Columbus

The first recorded celebration of Columbus Day on October 12 was in New York City in 1792, although more extensive festivities began among Italian-Americans in the late nineteenth century, and the day was made a U.S. federal holiday in 1937. The view of Columbus in these celebrations was heroic and triumphant: Columbus was the first "modern man" who ventured into the unknown just to find out what was there and stuck to his dreams despite the ridicule and scorn of his contemporaries. In the early twentieth century, several countries in Latin America began celebrating October 12 as *Dia de la Raza* ("day of the race"), commemorating the blending of European and indigenous cultures in the formation of a mixed-race society. Both holidays have more recently been sharply contested. Events in 1992 marking the 500th anniversary of Columbus's first voyage ranged from celebratory television specials and re-creations of the voyages to funerals for indigenous cultures and protests at statues of Columbus in Europe and the Americas. Some communities have renamed October 12 "Indigenous People's Day," and in 2002 Venezuela officially renamed Dia de la Raza *Día de la Resistencia Indígena* (Day of Indigenous Resistance). Even those who continue to sponsor parades now tend to recognize the mixed effects of Columbus's voyages, and the less attractive qualities of his character.

month of January, your Highnesses commanded me to go with an adequate fleet to those parts of India. In return you granted me great favors bestowing on me the titles of Don and High Admiral of the Ocean Sea and Viceroy and perpetual governor of such islands and mainland as I should discover and win or should in future be discovered and won in the Ocean Sea.

About five weeks after setting sail from the Canary Islands, Columbus's ships landed at an island in the Caribbean, which he named San Salvador, Spanish for Holy Savior. He was certain that he had reached an island off Asia, and called the inhabitants, who were members of the Taino people, "Indians," because he thought he was in the Indies, a word Europeans used for the islands of southeast Asia. He explored numerous islands for several months and then set off again for Spain. In a letter to the king and queen, Columbus marveled at the plants and birds he had seen, and also described the indigenous people. Columbus claimed the island for Spain, and took several captured Tainos with him back to Spain, where he was greeted in triumph by Isabella and Ferdinand. The letter that he wrote to the monarchs—sent by messenger from the dock in Lisbon so that it would arrive at their court just before he did—was quickly published, first in Spanish and then in many other languages, and news of the voyage spread throughout Europe.

On my arrival at that sea, I had taken some Indians by force from the first island that I came to, in order that they might learn our language, and communicate to us what they knew respecting the country; which plan succeeded excellently, and was a great advantage to us, for in a short time, either by gestures and signs, or by words, we were able to understand each other.... The inhabitants of both sexes in this island, and in all the others which I have seen, or of which I have received information, go always naked as they were born, with the exception of some of the women, who use a covering leaf, or small bough, or an apron of cotton which they prepare for that purpose. None of them, as I have already said, are possessed of any iron, neither have they weapons, being unacquainted with, and indeed incompetent to use them, not from any deformity of body (for they are well-formed), but because they are timid and full of fear. They carry however in lieu of arms, canes dried in the sun, on the ends of which they fix heads of dried wood sharpened to a point.... As soon however as they see that they are safe, and have laid aside all fear, they are very simple and honest, and exceedingly liberal with all they have; none of them refusing any thing he may possess when he is asked for it, but on the contrary inviting us to ask them. They exhibit a great love towards all others in preference to themselves: they also give objects of great value for trifles, and content themselves with very little or nothing in return.

In 1493, less than two months after Columbus returned, Pope Alexander VI (who was Spanish) issued a papal bull giving Ferdinand and Isabella the authority over all the lands west of a line near the Azores Islands in the Atlantic. The papal decree made no mention of Portugal, but the Portuguese king immediately began negotiations with the Spanish monarchs, and in 1494 the two nations agreed in the Treaty of Tordesillas on a line of demarcation about 1,000 miles west of that set by the pope. This ran right through South America, although no one knew it yet.

Among other works well pleasing to the Divine majesty and cherished of our heart, this assuredly ranks highest, that in our times especially the Catholic faith and the Christian religion be exalted and be everywhere increased and spread, that the health of souls be cared for and that barbarous nations be overthrown and brought to the faith itself . . . you have purposed with the favor of divine clemency to bring under your sway the said mainlands and islands with their residents and inhabitants to bring them to the Catholic faith. . . . And, in order that you may enter upon so great an undertaking with greater readiness and heartiness endowed with the benefit of our apostolic favor, we, of our own accord, . . . give, grant, and assign to you and your heirs and successors, kings of Castile and Leon, forever, together with all their dominions, cities, camps, places, and villages, and all rights, jurisdictions, and appurtenances, all islands and mainlands found and to be found, discovered and to be discovered towards the west and south, by drawing and establishing a line from

In 1507, the German mapmaker Martin Waldseemüller made a large map of the world, shown here, the first map to use the word "America" for newly-discovered lands. At that point Waldseemüller and others thought that the Florentine merchant and explorer Amerigo Vespucci had been the first to reach these lands, basing this on Vespucci's extensive descriptions of his voyages. By just a few years later, they knew that Columbus had been there first. They wanted to omit "America" from future maps, but the name had already stuck.

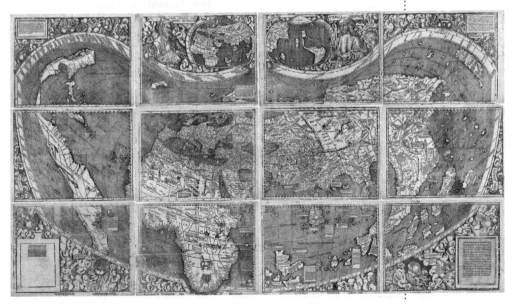

the Arctic pole, namely to the north, to the Antarctic pole . . . . You should appoint to the aforesaid mainlands and islands worthy, God-fearing, learned, skilled, and experienced men, in order to instruct the aforesaid inhabitants and residents in the catholic faith and train them in good morals.

The Impact of European Voyages in America and Africa

Although Columbus never gained the great riches he had hoped for, he did set the pattern for European colonization in much of what Europeans termed the "New World." Using gunpowder weapons and horses, European soldiers defeated indigenous peoples, including the powerful Aztec and Inca Empires. Spanish and Portuguese authorities established territorial states, not just fortresses as they did in Africa and India. They supported missionaries who attempted to convert native peoples, first preaching in Spanish and gradually in local languages as well. European diseases such as measles, mumps, bubonic plague, influenza, and smallpox, against which natives of the Americas had no resistance, killed thousands in the Caribbean and millions in Mesoamerica. The Spanish friar Bernardino de Sahagún included accounts of the European conquests and the devastating effects of disease in Mexico told to him by native peoples in his twelve-volume book describing and depicting Aztec life compiled between 1540 and 1585. This massive work, written mostly in the language of the Aztecs and with hundreds of illustrations, eventually ended up in the Medici family library in Florence, and so is referred to as the "Florentine Codex."

A great plague broke out here in Tenochtitlán [the capital of the Aztec Empire]. It began to spread during the thirteenth months and lasted for seventy days, striking everywhere in the city and killing a vast number of our people. Sores erupted on our faces, our breasts, our bellies; we were covered with agonizing sores from head to foot.

The illness was so dreadful that no one could walk or move. The sick were so utterly helpless that they could only lie on their beds like

A drawing from the late sixteenth century by an indigenous artist of the Spanish conquest of the Aztec Empire shows the conquistador Hernan Cortés seated in a chair, with the native woman who translated for him, generally known as La Malinche, standing beside him. Chiefs present tribute of food, gold, and parrots, and the military might of Spanish soldiers and their native allies literally stands behind Cortés's power.

corpses, unable to move their limbs or even their heads. They could not lie face down or roll from one side to the other. If they did move their bodies, they screamed with pain. A great many died from the plague, and many others died of hunger. They could not get up to search for food, and everyone else was too sick to care for them, so they starved to death in their beds.

Some people came down with a milder form of the disease; they suffered less than the others and made a good recovery. But they could not escape entirely. Their looks were ravaged, for wherever a sore broke out, it gouged an ugly pockmark in the skin. And a few of the survivors were left completely blind.

European authorities attempted to force native peoples to work for them raising crops and in Mexico and Peru mining gold and silver. Many died or ran away, and Europeans began to import enslaved Africans, particularly to work on huge sugar plantations. Columbus saw the possibilities of wealth from sugar firsthand when he lived on the Portuguese Atlantic islands, and he took sugar cane cuttings to the Caribbean on his second voyage. Spanish landowners on the Caribbean islands began to plant and process sugar, and soon Portuguese landowners in Brazil did as well. Sugar requires the back-breaking labor of many workers, and the cheapest source of those workers was the slave trade that already existed along the West African coast. Slave traders from coastal areas went further and further inland to capture, buy, or trade for more and more slaves. In 1526, King Afonso I of Kongo, who ruled the largest state in West Africa and had converted to Christianity, wrote a letter to the king of Portugal asking him to stop the slave trade. Afonso's request was not fulfilled, however, and the slave trade grew steadily, eventually taking millions of people from Africa.

Sir, Your Highness should know how our Kingdom is being lost in so many ways . . . merchants are taking every day our natives, sons of the land and the sons of our noblemen and vassals and our relatives, because the thieves and men of bad conscience grab them wishing to have the things and wares of this Kingdom which they are ambitious of; they grab them and get them to be sold; and so great, Sir, is the corruption and licentiousness that our country is being completely depopulated, and Your Highness should not agree with this nor accept it as in your service. And to avoid it we need from those [your] Kingdoms no more than some priests and a few people to teach in schools, and no other goods except wine and flour for the holy sacrament. That is why we beg of Your Highness to help and assist us in this matter, commanding your factors that they should not send here either merchants or wares, because it is our will that in these Kingdoms there should not be any trade of slaves nor outlet for them. . . .

The Triangle Trade

Ships that brought slaves to the Caribbean and Brazil (and later, in smaller numbers, to North America and the rest of South America) took sugar and molasses to Europe, and brought European cloth and manufactured goods to Africa and the Caribbean. Or they took flour and lumber from North America to tropical plantations, and carried molasses on the way back, which was processed into rum. West Africa, Europe, and the Caribbean formed three points in what is often called the "triangle trade" of the Atlantic. Any leg of this triangle offered opportunities. The slave trade by itself did not bring spectacular profits, but the plantation system was an essential part of a business network that provided steadily increasing wealth for European merchants and investors.

Moreoever, Sir, in our Kingdoms there is another great inconvenience which is of little service to God, and this is that many of our people, keenly desirous as they are of the wares and things of your Kingdoms, which are brought here by your people, and In order to satisfy their voracious appetite, seize many of our people, freed and exempt men, and very often it happens that they kidnap even noblemen and the sons of noblemen, and our relatives, and take them to be sold to the white men who are in our Kingdoms; and for this purpose they have concealed them; and others are brought during the night so that they might not be recognized.

And as soon as they are taken by the white men they are immediately ironed and branded with fire, and when they are carried to be embarked, if they are caught by our guards' men the whites allege that they have bought them but they cannot say from whom, so that it is our duty to do justice and to restore to the freemen their freedom.

Thinking about the Americas in Europe

Voyages to the Americas enhanced the wealth and power of many Europeans, but they also posed an intellectual challenge for educated people steeped in the culture of the Renaissance. Amerigo Vespucci put the problem succinctly in a letter written in 1502 to one of the leaders of Florence.

I ... discovered much continental land and innumerable islands, and great part of them inhabited ... there is no mention made by the ancient writers of them, I believe, because they had no knowledge thereof.

But how could "ancient writers," by which Vespucci means the classical Greeks and Romans so revered by Renaissance thinkers, not have known about the Americas and their inhabitants? Did this mean their knowledge was faulty? The presence of New World peoples also challenged Christian teachings. If the Flood described in the Old Testament truly covered the whole world, then the Indians must be descendents of Noah. But when and how did they get there? Were they the same as Europeans, or more like animals or children? If they were people just like Europeans, why did European rulers have the right to claim ownership of their land and enslave them? In 1537, Pope Paul III declared that the indigenous people of the Americas were rational beings with souls, but this did not settle the issue. In 1550, Charles V, the Emperor and King of Spain with author-

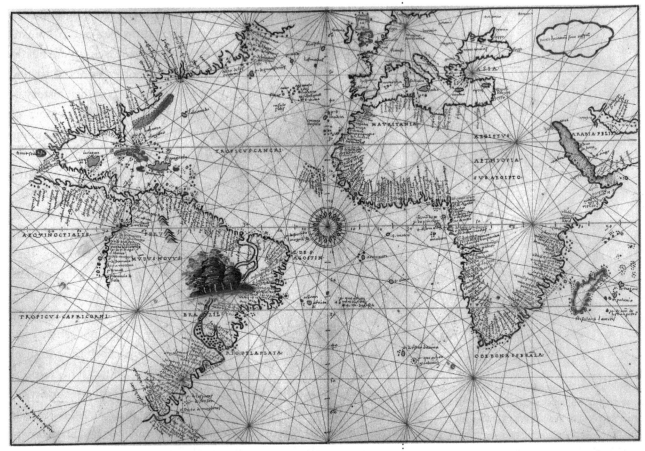

This sailors' map from 1544 shows the coasts of Africa, the Caribbean, and northern South America extremely accurately, indicating how thoroughly these had been explored by Portuguese and Spanish ships. The mapmaker shows trees in South America to highlight the most important export of the area at that point: the reddish logs of certain species of trees, used in Europe to make red dye for luxury textiles. Portuguese sailors who found these trees called them "brasil" from the Portuguese word for glowing embers, from which the country of Brazil later took its name.

ity over the largest colonies in the New World, ordered a public debate before a panel of theologians and judges. Juan Ginés de Sepúlveda, a scholar and Church official who spent his whole life in Spain, took one side, arguing the position he had laid out in 1544 in *A Treatise on the Just Causes of War against the Indians.*

It is established then, in accordance with the authority of the most eminent thinkers, that the dominion of prudent, good, and humane men over those of contrary dispositions is just and natural. . . .

[Therefore,] you can easily understand . . . if you are familiar with the character and moral code of the two peoples, that it is with perfect right that the Spaniards exercise their dominion over those barbarians of the New World and its adjacent islands. For in prudence, talent, and every kind of virtue and human sentiment they are as inferior to the Spaniards as children are to adults, or women to men, or the cruel and inhumane to the very gentle, or the excessively intemperate to the continent and moderate . . .

Compare these [Spanish] qualities of prudence, skill, magnanimity, moderation, humanity, and religion with those of those little

Girolamo Benzoni, an Italian merchant who was a member of a Spanish expedition in Central America, reclines in a hammock (a Native American invention), discussing Christianity with a local ruler while servants bustle about. This engraving by Theodor de Bry appeared in Benzoni's account of the New World published in 1565. In it, he portrays Native Americans as peaceful and the Spanish as vicious and violent, so that the book was soon used by those who opposed Spanish interests in the New World.

men [of America] in whom one can scarcely find any remnants of humanity. They not only lack culture but do not even use or know about writing or preserve records of their history—save for some obscure memory of certain deeds contained in painting. They lack written laws and their institutions and customs are barbaric. . . . Do not believe that their life before the coming of the Spaniards was one of peace, of the kind that poets sang about. On the contrary, they made war with each other almost continuously, and with such fury that they considered a victory to be empty if they could not satisfy their prodigious hunger with the flesh of their enemies . . . But in other respects they are so cowardly and timid that they can scarcely offer any resistance to the hostile presence of our side, and many times thousands and thousands of them have been dispersed and have fled like women, on being defeated by a small Spanish force scarcely amounting to one hundred. . . . How can we doubt that these people—so uncivilized, so barbaric, contaminated with so many impieties and obscenities—have been justly conquered by such an excellent, pious, and just king, as Ferdinand was and as the Emperor Charles is now, and by a nation excellent in every kind of virtue, with the best law and best benefit for the barbarians? Prior to the arrival of the Christians they had the nature, customs, religion, and practice of evil sacrifice as we have explained. Now, on receiving with our rule our writing, laws, and morality, imbued with the Christian religion, having shown themselves to be docile to the missionaries that we have sent them, as many have done, they are as different from their primitive condition as civilized people are from barbarians, or as those with sight from the blind, as the inhuman from the meek, as the pious from the impious, or to put it in a single phrase, in effect, as men from beasts.

On the other side of the debate was Bartolomé de Las Casas, who had first gone to the New World in pursuit of his fortune on one of Columbus's voyages, but later became a missionary working with indigenous people and eventually a bishop in Mexico. Las Casas had already made several trips to the Spanish court advocating better treatment of New World peoples. Las Casas's arguments against Sepúlveda were published in 1551, soon after the debate, as *In Defense of the Indians*. The judges in the debate decided that neither side was the winner, but more people in Europe accepted Sepúlveda's line of argument than Las Casas's, an assessment that shaped European colonialism and imperialism for centuries.

From the fact that the Indians are barbarians it does not necessarily follow that they are incapable of government and have to be ruled by others, except to be taught about the Catholic faith and to be admitted to the holy sacraments. They are not ignorant, inhuman, or bestial. Rather, long before they had heard the word Spaniard they had properly organized states, wisely ordered by excellent laws, religion, and custom. They cultivated friendship and, bound together in common fellowship, lived in populous cities in which they wisely administered the affairs of both peace and war justly and equitably, truly governed by laws that at very many points surpass ours, and could have won the admiration of the sages of Athens.... The Indian race is not that barbaric, nor are they dull witted or stupid, but they are easy to teach and very talented in learning all the liberal arts, and very ready to accept, honor, and observe the Christian religion and correct their sins (as experience has taught) once priests have introduced them to the sacred mysteries and taught them the word of God. They have been endowed with excellent conduct, and before the coming of the Spaniards, as we have said, they had political states that were well founded on beneficial laws.

Furthermore, they are so skilled in every mechanical art that with every right they should be set ahead of all the nations of the known world on this score, so very beautiful in their skill and artistry are the things this people produces in the grace of its architecture, its painting, and its needlework.... Their skillfully fashioned works of superior refinement awaken the admiration of all nations, because works proclaim a man's talent....

In the liberal arts that they have been taught up to now, such as grammar and logic, they are remarkably adept. With every kind of music they charm the ears of their audience with wonderful sweetness. They write skillfully and quite elegantly, so that most often we are at a loss to know whether the characters are hand written or printed ... I have seen [this] with my eyes, felt with my hands, and heard with my own ears while living a great many years among those peoples....

It is clear that the basis for Sepúlveda's teaching that these people are uncivilized and ignorant is worse than false.

Dürer's View of Aztec Art

Right after the conquest of the Aztec Empire, Cortés shipped Aztec art back to Europe, where it was seen and appreciated by Renaissance artists, including Albrecht Dürer. His comments about it in his diary from 1521 reflect a view of the people who made it similar to that of Las Casas: "All the days of my life I have seen nothing that rejoiced my heart so much as these things, for I have seen among them wonderful works of art, and I marveled at the subtle intellect of men in foreign lands."

Timeline

ca. 1300
Craft guilds first develop

1302
Pope Boniface VIII declares the papacy supreme in all things

1337–1453
Hundred Years' War

1347
Black Death spreads to Europe

1349
King Edward III of England freezes wages and prices

ca. 1350
Petrarch develops ideas of humanism

1381
English Peasants' Revolt

1415
Prince Henry of Portugal begins to sponsor ships along the African coast

1434–1737
Medici family in power in Florence

1490s
Leonardo da Vinci paints *The Last Supper*

1492
Ferdinand and Isabella of Spain conquer Granada, expel practicing Jews from Spain, and agree to support Columbus's first voyage

1494
Treaty of Tordesillas divides the world into Spanish and Portuguese zones

1497
Vasco da Gama's fleet reaches India

1501–1504
Michelangelo sculpts the *David* in Florence

1511
Erasmus publishes *The Praise of Folly*

1513
Machiavelli publishes *The Prince*

1516
Thomas More publishes *Utopia*

1517
Martin Luther writes the ninety-five theses on the power of indulgences

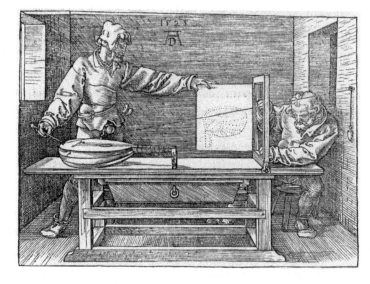

1520s

Sections of Germany, Switzerland, and other parts of central and northern Europe become Protestant; religious wars begin

1524–1526

Peasants' War in Germany

1525

Luther marries Katharina von Bora

1528

Castiglione publishes *The Courtier*

1530s

Henry VIII ends the authority of the pope in England

1534

Ignatius Loyola founds the Jesuits

1536

John Calvin publishes *The Institutes of the Christian Religion*

1537

Pope Paul III declares the indigenous people of the Americas to be rational beings with souls

1537–1541

Michelangelo paints *The Last Judgment* in the Sistine Chapel in Rome

1542

Pope Paul III establishes the Roman Inquisition

1543

Copernicus publishes *On the Revolution of the Heavenly Bodies*, which argues that the planets revolve around the sun

1545–1563

Council of Trent

1555

Louise Labé publishes her poems

1562

Teresa of Ávila founds a convent in her native city of Ávila

ca. 1600

Shakespeare writes *Hamlet*

1610

Galileo publishes the *Starry Messenger*

Further Reading

The Later Middle Ages: Overviews

Aberth, John. *From the Brink of the Apocalypse: Confronting Famine, War, Plague, and Death in the Later Middle Ages.* London: Routledge, 2001.

Allmand, Christopher. *The Hundred Years War: England and France at War, ca. 1300–1450.* Rev. ed. Cambridge: Cambridge University Press, 2005.

Herlihy, David. *The Black Death and the Transformation of the West.* Cambridge, MA: Harvard University Press, 1997.

Jordan, William Chester. *The Great Famine: Northern Europe in the Early Fourteenth Century.* Princeton, NJ: Princeton University Press, 1996.

Karras, Ruth Mazo. *From Boys to Men: Formations of Masculinity in Late Medieval Europe.* Philadelphia: University of Pennsylvania Press, 2002.

Keen, Maurice. *English Society in the Later Middle Ages, 1348–1500.* New York: Penguin, 1990.

Lehfeldt, Elizabeth, ed. *The Black Death.* Boston: Houghton Mifflin, 2005.

Tuchman, Barbara. *A Distant Mirror: The Calamitous Fourteenth Century.* New York: Random House, 1978.

The Renaissance: Overviews

Brotton, Jerry. *The Renaissance: A Very Short Introduction.* Oxford: Oxford University Press, 2006.

Burke, Peter. *The Italian Renaissance: Culture and Society in Europe.* Princeton, NJ: Princeton University Press, 1986.

Cohen, Elizabeth S., and Thomas V. Cohen. *Daily Life in Renaissance Italy.* New York: Greenwood, 2008.

Hay, Denys. *Italy in the Age of the Renaissance, 1380–1530.* New York: Longman, 1989.

Jardine, Lisa. *Worldly Goods: A New History of the Renaissance.* New York: Norton, 1996.

Konstam, Angus. *Historical Atlas of the Renaissance.* New York: Checkmark Books, 2004.

Larsen, Anne, Diana Robin, and Carole Levin, eds. *Encyclopedia of Women in the Renaissance: Italy, France and England.* Santa Barbara, CA: ABC-Clio, 2007.

Martines, Lauro. *Power and Imagination: City-States in Renaissance Italy.* New York: Vintage, 1980.

Sider, Sandra. *Handbook to Life in Renaissance Europe.* New York: Oxford University Press, 2005.

Speake, Jennifer, and Thomas G. Bergin. *Encyclopedia of the Renaissance and Reformation.* Rev. ed. New York: Facts on File, 2004.

The Protestant and Catholic Reformations: Overviews

Bireley, Robert. *The Refashioning of Catholicism: A Reassessment of the Counter Reformation.* Washington, DC: Catholic University Press of America, 1999.

Bossy, John. *Christianity in the West, 1500–1700.* New York: Oxford University Press, 1985.

Collinson, Patrick. *The Reformation: A History.* New York: Modern Library, 2004.

Hillerbrand, Hans, ed. *The Oxford Encyclopedia of the Reformation.* 4 vols. New York: Oxford University Press, 1996.

Hsia, R. Po-Chia. *The World of Catholic Renewal, 1540–1770.* Cambridge: Cambridge University Press, 1998.

O'Malley, John W. *Trent and All That: Renaming Catholicism in the Early Modern Era.* Cambridge, MA: Harvard University Press, 2000.

Rublack, Ulinka. *Reformation Europe.* Cambridge: Cambridge University Press, 2005.

Wright, Anthony D. *The Counter-Reformation: Catholic Europe and the Non-Christian World.* 2nd ed. Aldershot: Ashgate, 2005.

Biographies

Fernández-Armesto, Felipe. *Columbus.* Oxford: Oxford University Press, 1992.

Frieda, Leonie. *Catherine de Medici: Renaissance Queen of France.* New York: Harper Perennial, 2006.

Gordon, Bruce. *John Calvin.* New Haven, CT: Yale University Press, 2009.

Guy, John. *Thomas More.* Oxford: Oxford University Press, 2000.

King, Ross. *Machiavelli: Philosopher of Power.* New York: Harper, 2006.

Medwick, Cathleen. *Teresa of Avila: The Progress of a Soul.* New York: Image, 2001.

Nicholl, Charles. *Leonardo: Flights of the Mind.* New York: Viking, 2004.

Tracy, James. *Erasmus of the Low Countries.* Berkeley: University of California Press, 1997.

Wallace, William. *Michelangelo: The Artist, the Man, and His Times.* Cambridge: Cambridge University Press, 2009.

Economic and Social Developments

Brotton, Jerry. *The Renaissance Bazaar: From the Silk Road to Michelangelo.* New York: Oxford University Press, 2004.

Duplessis, Robert S. *Transitions to Capitalism in Early Modern Europe.* Cambridge: Cambridge University Press, 1997.

Hunt, Edwin S., and James M. Murray. *A History of Business in Medieval Europe, 1200–1550.* Cambridge: Cambridge University Press, 1999.

Wiesner-Hanks, Merry E. *Women and Gender in Early Modern Europe.* 3rd ed. Cambridge: Cambridge University Press, 2008.

Explorations and Colonialism

Bitterli, Urs. *Cultures in Conflict: Encounters Between European and Non-European Cultures, 1492–1800,* trans. Ritchie Robertson. New York: Polity Press, 1989.

Dathorne, O. R. *Imagining the World: Mythical Belief versus Reality in Global Encounters.* Westport, CT: Bergin and Garvey, 1994.

Elliott, J. H. *The Old World and the New, 1492–1650.* Cambridge: Cambridge University Press, 1972.

Fernández-Armesto, Felipe. *Before Columbus: Exploration and Colonization from the Mediterranean to the Atlantic, 1229–1492.* London: Macmillan Education, 1987.

Pérez-Mallaina, Pablo E. *Spain's Men of the Sea: Daily Life on the Indies Fleet in the Sixteenth Century,* trans. Carla Rahn Phillips. Baltimore, MD: Johns Hopkins University Press, 2005.

Phillips, William D., Jr., and Carla Rahn Phillips. *The Worlds of Christopher Columbus.* Cambridge: Cambridge University Press, 1992.

Scammell, Geoffrey Vaughn. *The First Imperial Age: European Overseas Expansion, ca. 1400–1715.* London: Unwin Hyman, 1989.

Schlesinger, Roger. *In the Wake of Columbus: The Impact of the New World on Europe, 1492–1650.* Wheeling, IL: Harlan Davidson, 1996.

Thornton, John. *Africa and Africans in the Making of the Atlantic World, 1400–1680.* Cambridge: Cambridge University Press, 1992.

Primary Sources

Baldassarri, Stefano Ugo, and Arielle Saiber, eds. *Images of Quattrocento Florence: Selected Writings in Literature, History, and Art.* New Haven, CT: Yale University Press, 2000.

Chojnacka, Monica, and Merry E. Wiesner-Hanks. *Ages of Woman, Ages of Man: Sources in European Social History, 1400–1750.* London: Longman, 2002.

Elmer, Peter, Nicholas Webb, and Roberta Wood, eds. *The Renaissance in Europe: An Anthology.* New Haven, CT: Yale University Press, 2000.

Janz, Denis. *A Reformation Reader.* Minneapolis, MN: Augsburg Fortress, 2002.

Karant-Nunn, Susan C., and Merry E. Wiesner-Hanks, eds. and trans. *Luther on Women: A Sourcebook.* Cambridge: Cambridge University Press, 2003.

Ross, James Bruce, and Mary Martin McLaughlin, eds. *The Portable Renaissance Reader.* New York: Penguin, 1978.

Renaissance Learning and Culture

Atlas, Allan W. *Renaissance Music: Music in Western Europe, 1400–1600.* New York: Norton, 1998.

Eisenstein, Elizabeth. *The Printing Press as an Agent of Change: Communications and Cultural Transformations in Early Modern Europe.* Cambridge: Cambridge University Press, 1979.

Grafton, Anthony, and Lisa Jardine. *From Humanism to the Humanities: Education and the Liberal Arts in Fifteenth and Sixteenth-Century Europe.* Cambridge, MA: Harvard University Press, 1986.

Holmes, George, ed. *Art and Politics in Renaissance Italy.* London: British Academy, 1993.

Johnson, Geraldine. *Renaissance Art: A Very Short Introduction.* New York: Oxford University Press, 2005.

Kent, F. W. *Lorenzo de' Medici and the Art of Magnificence.* Baltimore, MD: Johns Hopkins University Press, 2004.

King, Ross. *Brunelleschi's Dome: How a Renaissance Genius Reinvented Architecture.* New York: Penguin, 2000.

Lubkin, Gregory. *A Renaissance Court: Milan Under Galeazzo Maria Sforza.* Berkeley: University of California Press, 1994.

Nauert, Charles G., Jr. *Humanism and the Culture of Renaissance Europe.* 2nd ed. Cambridge: Cambridge University Press, 2006.

Parks, Tim. *Medici Money: Banking, Metaphysics, and Art in Fifteenth-Century Florence.* New York: Norton, 2005.

Social Issues and Popular Religion

Doran, Susan, and Christopher Durston. *Princes, Pastors and People: The Church and Religion in England, 1500–1700.* 2nd ed. London: Routledge, 2003.

Duffy, Eamon. *Voices of Morebath: Reformation and Rebellion in an English Village.* New Haven, CT: Yale University Press, 2001.

Harrington, Joel. *Reordering Marriage and Society in Reformation Germany*. Cambridge: Cambridge University Press, 1995.

Matheson, Peter, ed. *A People's History of the Reformation*. Minneapolis: Augsburg Fortress, 2007.

Monter, William E. *Calvin's Geneva*. New York: R. E. Krieger, 1975.

Shagan, Ethan. *Popular Politics and the English Reformation*. Cambridge: Cambridge University Press, 2003.

Theology and Intellectual Developments

Hendrix, Scott. *Luther*. Nashville, TN: Abingdon, 2009.

Levi, Anthony. *Renaissance and Reformation: The Intellectual Genesis*. New Haven, CT: Yale University Press, 2002.

O'Malley, John, S. J. *The First Jesuits*. Cambridge, MA: Harvard University Press, 1992.

Whitford, David. *Luther: A Guide for the Perplexed*. London: T & T Clark, 2010.

Websites

An American Ballroom Companion: Dance Instruction Manuals, ca. 1490–1920

http://memory.loc.gov/ammem/dihtml/divideos.html

A Library of Congress site on dance instruction manuals, with video clips of many Renaissance dance steps.

The Cely Papers

www.r3.org/bookcase/cely/index.html

Letters and memoranda from members of the Cely family, a very wealthy family of English wool merchants, 1475–1488.

Christian Classics Ethereal Library

www.ccel.org

Searchable versions of many works from the Church Fathers and links to many others, including works by John Calvin, Ignatius Loyola, Martin Luther, Teresa of Ávila, and many others.

Early Americas Digital Archive (EADA)

www.mith2.umd.edu/eada/intro.php

A collection of electronic texts originally written in or about the Americas from 1492 to about 1820. EADA invites contributions by scholars in any discipline, so the number of texts is steadily growing. Also includes links to other works by early American authors on the web. Sponsored by the Maryland Institute for Technology in the Humanities.

Early Modern Jewish History Resources

www.earlymodern.org

Collection of documents pertaining to Jewish life in early modern Europe in the original language and English translation, with introductions and discussion by noted scholars. Sponsored by Wesleyan University and the Joseph and Rebecca Meyerhoff Center for Jewish Studies at the University of Maryland.

Early Modern Women Database

www.lib.umd.edu/ETC/LOCAL/emw/emw.php3

Megasite with links to many original sources and other resources about women. Maintained by the University of Maryland libraries.

English History Tudor Sources

http://englishhistory.net/tudor/primary.html

Several dozen accounts, speeches, letters, and other sources on Tudor England.

Erasmus Text Project

http://smith2.sewanee.edu/erasmus

Includes several of Erasmus's works in English translation, and the *Praise of Folly* in both Latin and English.

Hanover Historical Texts Project

http://history.hanover.edu/project.html

Hanover University's site with many historical texts, including (in English) works by Petrarch and Martin Luther, English royal acts and decrees, and other documents from the Protestant and Catholic Reformations.

Internet Modern History Sourcebook

www.fordham.edu/halsall/mod/modsbook.html

Hundreds of sources on all aspects of modern history, organized by topic. Established by Paul Halsall and sponsored by Fordham University, the site also includes sourcebooks for ancient, medieval, women's, African, East Asia, Indian, Islamic, Jewish, LGBT, and global history, and the history of science.

Letters of Philip II, King of Spain, 1592–1597

www.lib.byu.edu/~rdh/phil2

Brigham Young University Library site with 153 letters in Spanish from King Philip II to Diego de Orellana, his representative on the northern coast, and others, written after the defeat of the Spanish Armada. Facsimiles with Spanish transcription and English summaries.

Luminarium

www.luminarium.org

Works of many English writers, 1350 through 1660.

Medici Archive Project

www.medici.org

This project is creating a database for researching the nearly three million letters (in 6,429 bound volumes, more than a kilometer of shelf space) held by the archives on the Medici Grand Dukes of Tuscany, who ruled Florence from 1537 to 1743. An Arts and Humanities index is now nearing completion, and the site has translations of about thirty "document highlights" currently available.

Medici Archives Jewish Collection

www.medici.org/jewish-history

The Medici Granducal Archive houses thousands of letters relevant to Jewish affairs throughout Europe and the Mediterranean World in the sixteenth, seventeenth, and early eighteenth centuries. Every Jewish document in the archive is now being registered in a customized database; eventually there will be full transcriptions in the original languages accompanied by summaries in English. Some especially interesting documents are posted on the website now.

Mr. William Shakespeare and the Internet

http://shakespeare.palomar.edu

Megasite with links to Shakespeare resources available on the Internet.

Other Women's Voices: Translations of Women's Writing Before 1700

http://home.infionline.net/~ddisse

Website created and maintained by Dorothy Disse with substantial excerpts from more than 120 writings from around the world. About half of them come from the period between 1400 and 1700.

Pico della Mirandola Project

www.brown.edu/Departments/Italian
_Studies/pico

A joint project of Brown University and the University of Bologna featuring texts and critical apparatus of several of Mirandola's works, some with English translations.

Printing in England from William Caxton to Christopher Barker (1479–1599)

http://special.lib.gla.ac.uk/exhibns/
printing/index.html

Online version of an exhibition at the University of Glasgow library of books relating to early printing that includes many visual sources.

Project Wittenberg

http://iclnet.org/pub/resources/text/
wittenberg/wittenberg-home.html

Concordia Theological Seminary's site devoted to the life and works of Martin Luther, with the largest online collection of Luther's writings in English, and many of his works in the original German or Latin.

Renaissance Festival Books

www.bl.uk/treasures/festivalbooks/
homepage.html

253 digitized Renaissance festival books that describe the magnificent festivals and ceremonies that took place in Europe between 1475 and 1700.

Timeline of Art History

www.metmuseum.org/toah

A chronological, geographical, and thematic exploration of the history of art from around the world, as illustrated especially by the Metropolitan Museum of Art's collection. Includes numerous special topics sections on nearly every aspect of Renaissance art, and also on armor, anatomy, book production, musical instruments of all types, clothing, household furnishings, and political and economic developments.

Vistas: Visual Culture in Spanish America, 1520–1820

www.smith.edu/vistas

Bilingual website (Spanish and English) with thirty-one images of objects, buildings, sculptures, drawings, and paintings from all over Spanish America, prepared by Dana Leibsohn, Smith College, and Barbara Mundy, Fordham University.

Web Gallery of Art

www.wga.hu

A virtual museum and searchable database of European painting and sculpture from twelfth to mid-nineteenth centuries.

Text Credits

Main Text

13–14: Gabriele de Mussi, "Istoria de morbo sive mortalitate que fuit de 1348," in *The Black Death 1347*, George Deaux (New York: Weybright and Talley, 1969), 75.

14–16: Giovanni Boccaccio, *The Decameron*, trans. Mark Musa and Peter Bondanella (New York: W.W. Norton, 1977), 4, 5, 6, 8. © 1982 by Mark Musa and Peter Bondanella. Used by permission of W. W. Norton & Company, Inc.

17: "Report of Paris Medical Faculty," in *The Black Death*, Rosemary Horrox (Manchester, UK: Manchester University Press, 1994), 159–163.

17–18: "Medical Treatise, 15th century," in *The Black Death*, Rosemary Horrox (Manchester, UK: Manchester University Press, 1994), 194.

18–19: Theophilus of Milan, "Sermon, 14th century," in *The Black Death*, Rosemary Horrox (Manchester, UK: Manchester University Press, 1994), 149.

19–21: Jean de Venette, "Chronicle of the plague in the late 1340s," in *The Black Death*, Rosemary Horrox (Manchester, UK: Manchester University Press, 1994), 56–57.

22: King Edward III of England, "Statute of Laborers," in vol. 2, no. 5 of *Translations and Reprints from the Original Sources of European History*, eds. Edward P. Cheyney et al. (Philadelphia: University of Pennsylvania, 1902), 3–4.

23–24: John Froissart, vol. 2 of *Chronicles of England, France, Spain and the Adjoining Countries*, trans. Thomas Johnes, Esq. (London: William Smith, 1844), 240, 653.

24–25: Francesco Petrarca, "Sonnet XXIV," *The Sonnets, Triumphs, and Other Poems of Petrarch*, trans. Thomas Campbell (London: William Clowes and Sons, 1879), 253.

29: Benedetto Dei, "Letter on Florence," in *Florentine Merchants in the Age of the Medici*, Gertrude R. B. Richards (Cambridge, MA: Harvard University Press, 1932), 176.

30: Marsilio Ficino "Letter on Florence in 1492," in *The Portable Renaissance Reader*, eds. James Bruce Ross and Mary Martin McLaughlin (London: Penguin, 1953), 79. © 1953, renewed © 1981 by Viking Penguin Inc. Used by permission of Viking Penguin, a division of Penguin Group (USA) Inc.

30–32: Leonardo Bruni, *Life of Petrarch*, in *The Portable Renaissance Reader*, eds. James Bruce Ross and Mary Martin McLaughlin (London: Penguin, 1953), 127–129. © 1953, renewed © 1981 by Viking Penguin Inc. Used by permission of Viking Penguin, a division of Penguin Group (USA) Inc.

32–33: Francesco Petrarca, "Letter to a Friend, 1352," in *Petrarch, The First Modern Scholar and Man of Letters: A Selection From His Correspondence with Boccaccio and Other Friends, Designed to Illustrate the Beginnings of the Renaissance*, eds. and trans. James H. Robinson and Henry W. Rolfe (New York: G.P. Putnam's Sons, 1898), 164, 166.

33–35: Leon Battista Alberti, "Autobiography c. 1438," in *The Portable Renaissance Reader*, eds. James Bruce Ross and Mary Martin McLaughlin (London: Penguin, 1953), 480–486, 490. © 1953, renewed © 1981 by Viking Penguin Inc. Used by permission of Viking Penguin, a division of Penguin Group (USA) Inc.

35–37: Giovanii della Casa, *Galateo*, trans. Konrad Eisenbichler and Kenneth R. Bartlett (Toronto: Centre for Reformation and Renaissance Studies, 1986), 3–7, 10, 17, 18, 21, 53.

37–38: Baldassare Castiglione, illus., *The Courtier*, trans. Charles S. Singleton, ed. Edgar Mayhew (Garden City, NY: Doubleday, 1959), 206, 208, 211–212. © 1959 by Charles S. Singleton and Edgar de N. Mayhew. Used by permission of Doubleday, a division of Random House, Inc.

39: Niccolo Machiavelli, *The Prince and the Discourses*, trans. Luigi Ricci, rev. E. R. P. Vincent (New York: Random House, 1950), 53, 55, 56, 61.

43–44: Anatole France, ed. *Les oeuvres de Barnard Palissy*, in *The Portable Renaissance Reader*, eds. James Bruce Ross and Mary Martin McLaughlin (London: Penguin, 1953.), 577, 578. © 1953, renewed © 1981 by Viking Penguin Inc. Used by permission of Viking Penguin, a division of Penguin Group (USA) Inc.

45: *The Winter's Tale*, eds. Stephen Greenblatt and Andrew Gurr (New York: W.W. Norton, 1997), 4.4.88–118.

46–47: Leonardo da Vinci, "Notes on painting," in *The Literary Remains of Leonardo da Vinci*, ed. Jean Paul Richter (London: Sampson Low, 1883) in *The Portable Renaissance Reader*, eds. James Bruce Ross and Mary Martin McLaughlin (London: Penguin, 1953), 532–533. © 1953, renewed © 1981 by Viking Penguin Inc. Used by permission of Viking Penguin, a division of Penguin Group (USA) Inc.

48: Michelangelo, "Letter to Vittoria Colonna," in *The Complete Poetical Works of Henry Wadsworth Longfellow*, trans. Henry Wadsworth Longfellow (Boston: Houghton-Mifflin, 1903), 636.

48–49: Vittoria Colonna, *Sonnets for Michelangelo: A Bilingual Edition*, trans. Abigail Brundin (Chicago: University of Chicago Press, 2005), 137–138.

50–51: Pierre de Ronsard, *Songs and Sonnets of Pierre de Ronsard*, trans. Curtis Hidden Page (Boston: Houghton-Mifflin, 1903), 51, 68.

51: Louise Labé, "Sonnet I: Non havria Ulysse," in *Sonnets of Louise Labé 'La Belle Cordière'*, trans. Alta Lind Cook (Toronto: University of Toronto Press, 1950). © 1950 by University of Toronto Press. Reprinted with permission of the publisher.

52–53: Baldassare Castiglione, *The Courtier*, trans. Sir Thomas Hoby, in *The Portable Renaissance Reader*, eds. James Bruce Ross and Mary Martin McLaughlin (London: Penguin, 1953.), 424–426, 428. © 1953, renewed © 1981 by Viking Penguin Inc. Used by permission of Viking Penguin, a division of Penguin Group (USA) Inc.

54–55: Galileo Galilei, *The Sidereal Messenger*, trans. Edward Stafford Carlos, in *The Portable Renaissance Reader*, eds. James Bruce Ross and Mary Martin McLaughlin (London: Penguin, 1953), 609–611. © 1953, renewed © 1981 by Viking Penguin Inc. Used by permission of Viking Penguin, a division of Penguin Group (USA) Inc.

58: "Contract: Genoa, December 22, 1198," in *Medieval Trade in the Mediterranean World*, Robert S. Lopez and Harry Miskimin (New York: Columbia University Press, 1955), 182. © 1955 Columbia University Press. Reprinted with permission of the publisher.

68: Gene Brucker ed., *Two Memoirs of Renaissance Florence: The Diaries of Buonaccorse Pitti and Gregorio Dati*, trans. Julia Martines (Long Grove, IL: Waveland Press, 1967, reissued 1991), 118. All rights reserved. Reprinted by permission of Waveland Press, Inc.

68–69: Gene Brucker ed., *Two Memoirs of Renaissance Florence: The Diaries of Buonaccorse Pitti and Gregorio Dati*, trans. Julia Martines (Long Grove, IL: Waveland Press, 1967, reissued 1991), 120. All rights reserved. Reprinted by permission of Waveland Press, Inc.

69: "Proclamation: Genoa, September 1, 1408," in *Medieval Trade in the Mediterranean World*, Robert S. Lopez and Harry Miskimin (New York: Columbia University Press, 1955), 246. © 1955 Columbia University Press. Reprinted with permission of the publisher.

69–71: Gene Brucker ed., *Two Memoirs of Renaissance Florence: The Diaries of Buonaccorse Pitti and Gregorio Dati*, trans. Julia Martines (Long Grove, IL: Waveland Press, 1967, reissued 1991), 120, 130, 139. All rights reserved. Reprinted by permission of Waveland Press, Inc.

71–72: Alessandra Strozzi, *Selected Letters of Alessandra Strozzi: Bilingual Edition*, ed. and trans. Heather Gregory (Berkeley: University of California Press, 1997), 69.

72: Gene Brucker ed., *Two Memoirs of Renaissance Florence: The Diaries of Buonaccorse Pitti and Gregorio Dati*, trans. Julia Martines (Long Grove, IL: Waveland Press, 1967, reissued 1991), 113–114. All rights reserved. Reprinted by permission of Waveland Press, Inc.

73–74: Gene Brucker ed., *Two Memoirs of Renaissance Florence: The Diaries of Buonaccorse Pitti and Gregorio Dati*, trans. Julia Martines (Long Grove, IL: Waveland Press, 1967, reissued 1991), 121. All rights reserved. Reprinted by permission of Waveland Press, Inc.

74: Dino Compagna, "Song on Worthy Conduct," in *Medieval Trade in the Mediterranean World*, Robert S. Lopez and Harry Miskimin (New York: Columbia University Press, 1955), 425–426. © 1955 Columbia University Press. Reprinted with permission of the publisher.

74–76: Gene Brucker ed., *Two Memoirs of Renaissance Florence: The Diaries of Buonaccorse Pitti and Gregorio Dati*, trans. Julia Martines (Long Grove, IL: Waveland Press, 1967, reissued 1991), 124–125. All rights reserved. Reprinted by permission of Waveland Press, Inc. 76–77: "Letter of Venetian Merchants" in *Medieval Trade in the Mediterranean World*, Robert S. Lopez and Harry Miskimin (New York: Columbia University Press, 1955), 104. © 1955 Columbia University Press. Reprinted with permission of the publisher.

78: Podesta of Gavi, "Letter by Podesta of Gavi to Complain about the Hats of Angelino and Lazaro Nantua 1595," trans. Flora Cassen, New York University, accessed April 24, 2010, http://www.earlymodern.org/citation .php?citKey=77&docKey=e.

78–79: Elizabeth I, "Enforcing Statutes of Apparel," accessed April 24, 2010, http://www .elizabethan.org/sumptuary/who-wears-what.html.

79: "Spurriers' 1345 ordinances," in vol. 1 of *Readings in European History*, ed. and trans. James Harvey Robinson (Boston: Ginn, 1904), 409–411.

80–81: "Parisian apprenticeship contract," trans. Carole Loats, in *Ages of Woman, Ages of Man: Sources in European Social History, 1400–1750*, eds. Monica Chojnacka and Merry E. Wiesner-Hanks (London: Longman, 2002), 24.

82–83: "Unpublished goldsmiths' guild ordinance," trans. Merry Wiesner-Hanks, Rep. F5, no. 68/I, fol. 115., Quellen zur Nünbergische Geschichte, Nuremberg Stadtarchiv, Nuremberg. Author's translation.

83: "White-tawyers' guild ordinance," in vol. 2, no.1 of *Translations and Reprints from the Original Sources of European History*, ed. and trans. Edward P. Cheney (Philadelphia: University of Pennsylvania, 1894), 23.

89: Cameron Louise, *The Commonplace Book of Robert Reynes of Acle* (New York: Garland, 1980), in *Medieval Popular Religion 1000–1500: A Sourcebook*, ed. John Shinners (Peterborough, Ontario: Broadview Press, 1997), 369–370.

89–90: J. T. Fowler ed., *Extracts from the Account Rolls of the Abbey of Durham* (Durham, UK: Andres and Co., 1898), in *Medieval Popular Religion 1000–1500: A Sourcebook*, ed. John Shinners (Peterborough, Ontario: Broadview Press, 1997), 197.

90: George H. Tavard, "The Bull Unam Sanctam of Boniface VII," in *Papal Primacy and the Universal Church*, eds. Paul Empie and Thomas Austin Murphy (Minneapolis: Augsburg, 1974), 106–107.

91–92: Desiderius Erasmus, *The Praise of Folly* (Ann Arbor: University of Michigan Press, 1958), 98, 99, 100.

92–93: Albert of Mainz, *Instructio Summaria*, in *Martin Luther*, eds. Ernest Gordon Rupp and Benjamin Drewery (London: Edward Arnold and New York, St. Martin's Press, 1970), 13, 14, 17.

93–94: Martin Luther, "Ninety-five Theses," in vol. 31 of *Luther's Works*, ed. Harold J. Grimm (Philadelphia: Muhlenberg Press, 1957), 26, 27–28, 29, 30. Permission granted by Fortress Press.

94: Martin Luther, *Freedom of a Christian*, in vol. 31 of *Luther's Works*, ed. Harold J. Grimm (Philadelphia: Muhlenberg Press, 1957), 344–346. Permission granted by Fortress Press.

95: G. R. Potter, ed., *Huldrych Zwingli* (New York: St. Martin's Press, 1977), 29–30.

96: Henry VIII, "Act of Supremacy," in *Documents of the English Reformation*, ed. Gerald Bray (Minneapolis: Fortress Press, 1994), 113.

96: Leo X, "Exsurge Domine," in *Martin Luther*, eds. Ernest Gordon Rupp and Benjamin Drewery (London: Edward Arnold and New York, St. Martin's Press, 1970), 36.

97: Contarini and Carafa, "*Consilum de emedanda ecclesiae*," in *The Counter Reformation: Religion and Society in Early Modern Europe*, ed. Martin D. W. Jones (New York: Cambridge University Press, 1995), 45–46.

97–98: Paul III, "*Licet ab initio*," in *Readings in Christianity*, ed. Robert E. Van Voorst (New York: Wadsworth, 1997), 183–184.

98–99: Ignatius Loyola, "*Spiritual Exercises*," trans. Louis Puhl (Chicago: Loyola University Press, 1951), 157–160.

104: Martin Luther, "On Secular Authority," in *International Relations in Political Thought*, eds. Chris Brown, Terry Nardin and Nicholas Rengger (Cambridge, UK: Cambridge University Press, 2002), 209, 210.

105: "Trial of Michael Sattler," in *Spiritual and Anabaptist Writers*, eds. George H. Williams and Angel M. Mergal (Westminster, UK: John Knox Press, 1977), 181.

106: "Trial of Michael Sattler," in *Spiritual and Anabaptist Writers*, eds. George H. Williams and Angel M. Mergal (Westminster, UK: John Knox Press, 1977), 183.

106: Peter Walpot, *True Yieldedness and the Christian Community of Goods*, in *Early Anabaptist Spirituality*, ed. Daniel Liechty (New York: Paulist Press, 1994), 145, 191, 192.

107: "Trial of Michael Sattler," in *Spiritual and Anabaptist Writers*, eds. George H. Williams and Angel M. Mergal (Westminster, UK: John Knox Press, 1977), 183.

108: "Irish manuscript" in "The Irish Church in the Sixteenth Century," trans. Canice Mooney, *Irish Ecclesiastical Record* 99 (1963): 111.

109: "1564 French Pamphlet," in *The French Wars of Religion, 1562–1629*, Mack Holt (Cambridge, UK: Cambridge University Press, 1995), 62.

109–112: James Harvey Robinson and Merrick Whitcomb eds., "Twelve Articles," *Translations and Reprints from the Original Sources*, vol. II, no 6 (Philadelphia: University of Pennsylvania Press, 1902), 26–30.

112–113: Martin Luther, "Against the Robbing and Murdering Hordes of Peasants," in *Selected Writings of Martin Luther*, ed. Theodore G. Tappert (Minneapolis, MN: Fortress Press, 1967), 349–351.

114–115: Teresa of Avila, *The Life of St. Teresa of Jesus, of The Order of Our Lady of Carmel* (London: Thomas Baker; New York: Benzinger Bros., 1904), chapter 38, paragraphs 1, 3, 4, 6.

119: John Calvin, vol. 2 of *Institutes of the Christian Religion*, trans. Henry Beveridge (Edinburgh, UK: Calvin Translation Society, 1845), 534, 540.

121: John Calvin, "Ordinances for the Regulation of Churches," in vol. 3 of *Translations and Reprints from the Original Sources of European History*, ed. James Harvey Robinson (Philadelphia: University of Pennsylvania, 1902), 10–11.

121: "Registers of the Genevan Consistory, Thursday August 24, 1542" in *Reformation Christianity: A People's History of Christianity*, ed. Peter Mateson (Minneapolis, MN: Fortress Press, 2007), 42.

122–124: Martin Luther, "Sermon on Marriage," in *Luther on Women: A Sourcebook*, eds. and trans. Susan C. Karant-Nunn and Merry E. Wiesner-Hanks (Cambridge, UK: Cambridge University Press, 2003), 94–95.

124: Geminianus Monacensis, *Gesitlicher Weeg-Weiser gen Himmel* (Munich 1679), in *State of Virginity: Gender, Religion, and Politics in an Early Modern Catholic State*, trans. Ulrike Strasser (Ann Arbor: University of Michigan Press, 2004), 38.

125: J. Waterworth, ed. and trans., *The Council of Trent: The Canons and Decrees of the Sacred and Oecumenical Council of Trent* (London: Dolman, 1848), 213.

125–127: "Lutheran school ordinances," in *Luther's House of Learning: Indoctrination of the Young in the German Reformation*, trans. Gerald Strauss (Baltimore, MD, and London: Johns Hopkins University Press, 1978), 45–46, 131.

127–128: Santa María Amarante, "Libro de Visitas," trans. Allyson Poska, 24.1.13, fols. 9-10, Archivo Histórico Diocesano de Ourense, Ourense, Spain.

128–129: "Visitation report from Germany," in *Luther's House of Learning: Indoctrination of the Young in the German Reformation*, trans. Gerald Strauss (Baltimore, MD, and London: Johns Hopkins University Press, 1978), 283.

129–130: "Registers of the Genevan Consistory, Thursday, February 8, 1543," in *Reformation Christianity: A People's History of Christianity*, ed. Peter Mateson (Minneapolis: Fortress Press, 2007), 45.

130: Marc R. Forster, *The Counter-Reformation in the Villages: Religion and Reform in the Bishopric of Speyer, 1560–1700* (Ithaca, NY: Cornell University Press, 1992), 209.

130–131: "1606 petition from Ebsdorf parish," Stadtarchiv Marburg 41 153, in *Communal Christianity: The Life and Loss of a Peasant Vision in Early Modern Germany*, David Mayes (Leiden, Netherlands: Brill, 2004), 102. Author's translation.

136: Ludovico Guicciardini, *Descrittione di tutti i Paesi Bassi* (Antwerp, 1567) in *The Portable Renaissance Reader*, eds. James Bruce Ross and Mary Martin McLaughlin (London: Penguin, 1953), 196–197. © 1953, renewed © 1981 by Viking Penguin Inc. Used by permission of Viking Penguin, a division of Penguin Group (USA) Inc.

136–138: Gomes Eannes de Azurara, vol. 1 of *The Chronicle of the Discovery and Conquest of Guinea*, trans. Charles Raymond Beazely and Edgar Prestage (London: Hakluyt Society, 1896), 27–29 or 83–85.

138–139: Gaspar Correa, *The Three Voyages of Vasco da Gama*, trans. Henry E. J. Stanley (London: Hakluyt Society, 1869), 326–334.

140: Ludovico Guicciardini, *Descrittione di tutti i Paesi Bassi* (Antwerp, 1567) in *The Portable Renaissance Reader*, eds. James Bruce Ross and Mary Martin McLaughlin (London: Penguin, 1953), 186. © 1953, renewed © 1981 by Viking Penguin Inc. Used by permission of Viking Penguin, a division of Penguin Group (USA) Inc.

141–142: J. M. Cohen, trans., *The Four Voyages of Christopher Columbus* (Baltimore, MD: Penguin Books, 1969), 37–38.

142–143: R. H. Major, ed. and trans., *Select Letters of Christopher Columbus* (London: Hakluyt Society, 1857), 1–15.

143–144: Pope Alexandrer VI, *Inter Caetera*, in *European Treaties Bearing on the History of the United States and its Dependencies to 1648*, ed. Francis Gardener Davenport (Washington, DC: Carnegie Institute, 1917), 75–77.

144–145: Miguel León-Portilla, *The Broken Spears: The Aztec Account of the Conquest of Mexico*, 2nd ed. (Boston: Beacon Press, 1992), 90–91.

145–146: King Afonso I, "Letter to the king of Portugal," in *The African Past: Chronicles from Antiquity to Modern Times*, Basil Davidson (New York: Curtis Brown, Ltd., 1964), 123.

146: Amerigo Vespucci, "Letter to Florence, 1502," in *American Historical Documents*, ed. Charles W. Eliot (New York: Colliers, 1910), 31.

147–148: Juan Ginés de Sepúlveda, "Treatise on the Just Causes of War Against the Indians," in *The Spanish Tradition in America*, ed. Charles Gibson (New York: Harper and Row, 1968), 115, 118, 120. Compilation, introduction, notes, and translations by the editor © 1968 by Charles Gibson. Reprinted by permission of HarperCollins Publishers.

149: Bartolomé de Las Casas, *In Defense of the Indians*, ed. and trans. Stafford Poole (De Kalb: Northern Illinois University Press, 1974), 42–45.

Sidebars

15: Francesco Petrarca, "Letter on the plague," in *The Black Death 1347*, George Deaux (New York: Weybright and Talley, 1969), 94.

19: Jacob R. Marcus, *The Jew in the Medieval World: A Sourcebook, 315–1791* (New York: Jewish Publication Society, 1938), 48.

30: François Rabelais, *Gargantua and Pantagruel*, in vol. 2 of *Reading About the World*, 3rd ed., eds. Paul Brians, et al. (Fort Worth, TX: Harcourt Brace Custom, 1999), 23.

43: Andreas Vesalius, *On the Structure of the Human Body*, in *The Portable Renaissance Reader*, eds. James Bruce Ross and Mary Martin McLaughlin (London: Penguin, 1953), 564. © 1953, renewed © 1981 by Viking Penguin. Used by permission of Viking Penguin, a division of Penguin Group (USA) Inc.

53: Louise Labé, "Sonnet XII: Lut, compagnon de ma calamité," in *La Belle Cordière: Sonnets of Louise Labé*, trans. Alta Lind Cook (Toronto: University of Toronto Press, 1950). © 1950 by University of Toronto Press. Reprinted with permission of the publisher.

67: Ludovico Guicciardini, *Descrittione di tutti i Paesi Bassi* (Antwerp, 1567) in *The Portable Renaissance Reader*, eds. James Bruce Ross and Mary Martin McLaughlin (London: Penguin, 1953), 196–197, 187. © 1953, renewed © 1981 by Viking Penguin Inc. Used by permission of Viking Penguin, a division of Penguin Group (USA) Inc.

69: Jacob Fugger, "Letter to Charles V, 1519," in *The Portable Renaissance Reader*, eds. James Bruce Ross and Mary Martin McLaughlin (London: Penguin, 1953), 180. © 1953, renewed © 1981 by Viking Penguin Inc. Used by permission of Viking Penguin, a division of Penguin Group (USA) Inc.

106: "Anabaptist hymn: Jeronimus Segerz & wife song," in *Elisabeth's Manly Courage: Testimonials and Songs of Martyred Anabaptist Women in the Low Countries*, ed. and trans. Hermina Joldersma and Louis Grijp (Milwaukee, WI: Marquette University Press, 2001), 87. © 2001 Marquette University Press. Reprinted by permission of publisher.

121: "Motto of Nîmes consistory," in "Disciplina Nervus Ecclesiae: The Calvinist Reform of Morals at Nîmes," trans. Raymond A. Mentzer, *Sixteenth Century Journal* 18 (1987): 89.

124: "Tudor homily on marriage," in *The Two Books of Homilies*, Church of England (Oxford, UK: Oxford University Press, 1859), 505.

149: Albrecht Dürer, "Travel diary entry, 1521," in *Literary Remains of Albrecht Dürer*, W. M. Conway (Cambridge, UK: Cambridge University Press, 1889), 101–102.

Picture Credits

Acknowledgments

The author wishes to thank her students, who over her many years of teaching have continually reaffirmed her faith that using primary sources is the best way to encourage their understanding and enjoyment of history. She would also like to thank the editorial staff at Oxford University Press, including Nancy Toff, Karen Fein, Sonia Tycko, and DuanDuan Yang, for their encouragement and assistance as this project developed.

Index

References to illustrations and their captions are indicated by page numbers in **bold**.

About the Author

Merry Wiesner-Hanks is a Distinguished Professor of History at the University of Wisconsin-Milwaukee. She is the co-editor of the *Sixteenth Century Journal* and the author or editor of twenty books and many articles that have appeared in English, German, Italian, Spanish, Greek, Chinese, and Korean. These include *Early Modern Europe 1450–1789*, *Women and Gender in Early Modern Europe*, *Christianity and Sexuality in the Early Modern World: Regulating Desire, Reforming Practice*, and *Gender in History: Global Perspectives*. Her research has been supported by grants from the Fulbright and Guggenheim Foundations, among others. She has also written a number of source books for use in the college classroom, including *Discovering the Global Past*, a book for young adults, *An Age of Voyages, 1350–1600*, and a book for general readers, *The Marvelous Hairy Girls: The Gonzales Sisters and Their Worlds*, the story of a family of extremely hairy people who lived in Europe in the late sixteenth century. She has recently served as the Chief Reader for Advanced Placement World History and as the editor-in-chief of the forthcoming *Cambridge History of the World*.